GREAT INVENTORS
OF NEW YORK'S
CAPITAL DISTRICT

TIMOTHY STARR

Charleston | London

THE
History
PRESS

Published by The History Press
Charleston, SC 29403
www.historypress.net

Copyright © 2010 by Timothy Starr
All rights reserved

First published 2010

Manufactured in the United States

ISBN 978.1.59629.171.3

Library of Congress Cataloging-in-Publication Data

Starr, Timothy, 1971-
Great inventors of New York's Capital District / Timothy Starr.p. cm.
Includes bibliographical references.
ISBN 978-1-59629-171-3
1. Inventors--New York (State)--Albany Region--Biography. 2. Inventions--New York
(State)--Albany Region--History. I. Title.
T39.S925 2010
609.2'2747--dc22
2010018204

Notice: The information in this book is true and complete to the best of our knowledge. It is offered without guarantee on the part of the author or The History Press. The author and The History Press disclaim all liability in connection with the use of this book.

All rights reserved. No part of this book may be reproduced or transmitted in any form whatsoever without prior written permission from the publisher except in the case of brief quotations embodied in critical articles and reviews.

CONTENTS

CONTENTS

Contents

ACKNOWLEDGEMENTS

The author wishes to thank the following organizations for their contributions to this project:

Brookside Museum, Saratoga County Historical Society, Ballston Spa
Hudson-Mohawk Industrial Gateway, Troy
Efner City History Center, Schenectady
Rensselaer County Historical Society, Troy
New York State Archives, Albany
Waterford Museum and Cultural Center, Waterford
Library of Congress, American Memory Project
The United States Patent Office

The author would also like to thank his wife, Alison, and parents, Stephen and Elaine Starr, for all of their support.

INTRODUCTION

A ccording to several studies, fewer than one in every ten patents is ever used, and a much smaller percentage ever creates a significant profit for the inventor. Thomas Edison's famous quote that "success is 1 percent inspiration and 99 percent perspiration" holds true when it comes to inventions. Often, the idea is the easy part; the hard part is developing the idea into a product that is usable and then selling it to the right audience.

Inventors in New York State's Capital District during the nineteenth century seem to have enjoyed higher odds that their inventions would lead to fame and profit. This was an exciting time in the area's history, as the Industrial Revolution began in northeastern New York and swept the country, dramatically changing the lives of every American citizen. Thousands of patents were awarded to hundreds of gifted inventors prior to the Great Depression, bringing fame and prosperity to its industries.

The prominence of the Capital District at this time is somewhat difficult to imagine in the twenty-first century, when large portions of the country's population are now concentrated in the South and West. During the 1800s, only a few eastern cities such as New York, Philadelphia and Boston were larger than the Albany-Schenectady-Troy region. In fact, Upstate New York was considered to be one of the few centers of industry in the young country. Some historians contend that the Industrial Revolution began in Troy with the introduction of machinery for producing shirts and collars and the Bessemer process of manufacturing steel.

Today, the Capital District is heavily dependent upon the government, education and healthcare sectors for employment. However, during the

46X

S. G. DORR.
CLOTH SHEARING MACHINE.

Patented Oct. 20, 1792.

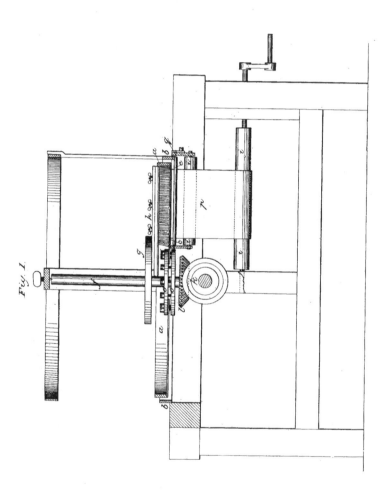

Samuel Dorr's "Cloth Shearing Machine," the Capital District's first patent.

1800s, it was one of the country's main transportation hubs and industrial centers. The completion of the Erie and Champlain Canals in the 1820s brought unprecedented trade traffic from the west and the north. The canals terminated at the Hudson River near Albany and Troy and provided easy access to New York City and its international harbor. Railroad building that commenced in the 1830s generated even more traffic, linking the region directly to the rest of the country.

In the years following the completion of the canals and railroads, large-scale industrial development took place in the cities of Albany, Watervliet, Cohoes, Schenectady and Troy. America's greatest inventor, Thomas Edison, decided to relocate his company's headquarters to Schenectady. Later renamed General Electric, it employed thirty thousand people at its height and supported many famous scientists. Cohoes became the center of the country's cotton and knitting industry after inventor Timothy Bailey installed his famous knitting machine at the Cohoes Falls. Troy became a major iron and steel manufacturer and pioneered the collar and cuff industry. Albany developed a wide range of industries, many of which were established or supported by inventors, such as the manufacture of stoves, agricultural machines, billiard balls and perforated paper.

A large number of the most successful businessmen of the era were inventors with at least one patent. Henry Burden, whose iron foundry occupied almost a mile of Hudson River waterfront, invented a horseshoe machine that provided the millions of horseshoes needed for the Union cavalry during the Civil War. Sanford Cluett invented a process for preshrinking fabrics that earned many millions of dollars and is still in use today. Foundry owner George Eddy invented a water valve that was used in almost every major city in the country. Lysander Button invented a wide range of important fire engine improvements that not only made his business a success but also advanced firefighting technology around the world. Thomas Wiles of Troy invented so many collar-processing machines that he established a business focused solely on manufacturing them.

Several inventions achieved worldwide fame. Before relocating elsewhere, George Westinghouse Jr. invented the railroad air brake in his father's Schenectady agricultural machine factory. This is still considered by many historians to be the most significant railroad-related invention in history. Arthur Knight developed the Schenectady Putter, which had a following among some of the top professional golfers in the United States. Albany scientist Joseph Henry pioneered several breakthroughs in long-distance communication that paved the way for Henry Morse to build the telegraph machine. Seth Wheeler invented the modern, perforated bathroom tissue that we use today. Inventors at General Electric pioneered many important advances in electrical technology that have affected the lives of hundreds of millions of people.

Nearly all of the inventors profiled in the following pages developed patents to protect their ideas. The patent system was written into Article 1, Section 8 of the Constitution, which states that one of the powers of Congress is: "To promote the progress of science and useful arts, by securing for limited times to authors and inventors the exclusive right to their respective writings and discoveries." Patent protection lasted for fourteen years (later expanded to twenty years), after which the idea was free for anyone to use.

The country's first patents were filed after the creation of the United States Patent Office in 1790. These patents were hand-written and unnumbered. Models of each patent had to be constructed and sent to Washington, where they were kept in a large storage building. During the War of 1812, the head of the Patent Office pleaded with British army officers to spare the collection, only for all ten thousand of them to be burned in 1836. Despite urgent calls by Congress for inventors to resubmit their patents, less than one-third of them have been replaced. These are now known as the X-patents and were numbered sequentially beginning with the letter X according to the date they were filed.

Inventors of the Capital District were awarded a number of patents before 1836, but many were never replaced after the fire. Schenectady's first patent was filed in 1808 by David Burt for a "hydrant for drawing water from aqueducts." Troy's first patent was awarded the following year to Moses Crafts for a horse-powered boat. Jonathan Minor was awarded Saratoga County's first patent in 1810 for a water wheel. The first patent filed in the entire Capital District was by Samuel Dorr of Albany, who invented a "wheel of knives" for shearing and raising the nap on cloths in 1792 (patent X00046).

Dorr's patent is also special because it was replaced after the patent office fire and is, in fact, the fourth-oldest surviving patent in the United States. Three other early inventors whose patents survive are included in this book: Barnabus Langdon, who invented various means for propelling boats; Eliphalet Nott, who invented the world's first anthracite coal–burning stove; and Henry Burden, who invented a famous horseshoe-making machine.

In this book, the word "patent" refers to the original or "utility" patents, of which about seven million have been awarded since 1836. However, there is also a class called "design patents," used to protect the appearance of an object. Several dozen design patents were filed in the Capital District, mainly for stoves and clothing.

Adjusted for inflation, the cost to file and maintain a patent has historically been about $5,000, including a patent search, filing an application, preparing an abstract and creating the drawings. This has no doubt discouraged many inventors from patenting their ideas. It is also another reason why so few inventors have more than a few patents, since it would only make sense to incur such costs if the inventions were successful. For example, Henry Miller of Waterford spent over $500,000 filing patents during his lifetime, but he was amply repaid by licensing them to local collar and cuff manufacturers and the Victor Talking Machine Company. Peter Dederick of Albany likely holds the record, spending the equivalent of over $1.5 million on patent protection for his agricultural machines.

A complete history of the area's inventions would be impossible to compress into one volume. Scientists working at Schenectady's General Electric alone have patented thousands of inventions. Therefore, certain boundaries as to what types of inventions and inventors would be included had to be followed. First, an arbitrary cutoff at the Great Depression was chosen. The time period of 1850 to 1930 was a distinct period in the Capital District. Manufacturing enterprises constituted a large share of the economy and employed tens of thousands of people. The industrial era ended in the early 1900s as manufacturing was moved west to be closer to natural resources and cheaper labor markets. This cutoff date also helps the readability factor of this book, as many of the most important inventions developed in the last seventy-five years were more technical in nature. Patents with titles such as "Composite Rotor Lamination for Use in Reluctance Hompolar and Permanent Magnet Machines" (No. 4,916,346) are not uncommon.

Second, this book greatly favors those inventions that succeeded in the marketplace. Although thousands of interesting patents have been awarded, they are often not compelling because they were never developed. Conversely, the hay presses of Peter Dederick, the fire engines of Lysander Button and the stoves of Philo Stewart were all manufactured locally and sold around the world.

Third, the geographic boundaries are confined to the immediate Capital District. While the term "Capital District" sometimes covers outlying counties such as Fulton, Montgomery and Warren, for the purposes of this book, it refers to the counties of Albany, Rensselaer and Schenectady. The extreme southern Saratoga County village of Waterford was also included due to its close ties and historical relationship with the cities of Cohoes and Troy.

One of the potential pitfalls in detailing inventors who have passed away long ago is the reliance on limited sources of material. Often there are only cryptic census records, subsidized biographies that tend to exaggerate an inventor's importance and limited corroboration from sources outside of the region. The latter sources may include lawsuits, advertisements and magazine articles that often do not contain vital information about the inventors themselves.

It is hoped that readers will be introduced to an era of the Capital District that has been all but forgotten. Most of the former factory buildings are vacant or were torn down long ago. The canals have fallen to disuse and in some areas were filled in, while railroad rights of way have lost their tracks and become walking trails. Nearly all of the inventions found here, although important and sometimes famous in their day, have been superseded by new technology. Often, it is only in books like this one that the legacy of innovation lives on.

WORKING THE LAND

When the first settlers arrived in Upstate New York in the early 1600s, the land did not look very inviting for farmers. A heavy growth of trees that would have to be cleared away before any type of sustainable agriculture could be established confronted the colonists. Other barriers included wild animals, severe northeastern winters and conflict with Native Americans and the British. In fact, it would be almost two centuries before area farms could produce enough crops to feed the local population and have enough left over to export to nearby cities in any quantity.

The output of crops after 1800 increased dramatically for several reasons. As an era of peace settled across the country, experienced farmers began to settle in the Albany area, bringing with them the knowledge needed to maintain sustainable farmlands. Fertilizer began to be used, which greatly increased the number of crops that could be supported in the soil as well as the crop yield per acre. Cash crops were introduced that could be sold for profit, such as hemp, flax, hops and broom corn. Farms quickly began to grow in number and in size. By 1880 there were nearly 3,500 farms in Albany County alone at an average size of ninety-two acres each.

The biggest factor in the physical growth of farms was the appearance of new labor-saving machinery. Several inventors in the Capital District patented hundreds of new types of machinery and improvements. Many of these were manufactured locally and sold around the country. Peter Dederick's hay press enabled local farmers to harvest and process ninety-five thousand tons of hay in 1880, while Lewis Aspinwall's improved potato planters and diggers had a hand in making potatoes the second-largest food crop in the region (after oats) with a total yield of nearly 500,000 bushels.

Although most agriculture-based inventions originated in Albany, Schenectady County could lay claim to important innovation as well. The works of George Westinghouse Sr. produced some of the most practical and sturdiest improved machinery in the area. James Covert's improved harnesses and snap hooks were so effective that they were manufactured and sold well into the twentieth century. The wire machines of John Griswold inspired the creation of the Northwestern Steel and Wire Company in Sterling, Illinois, which only suspended the manufacture of wire in 1998. Seth Wheeler not only invented a variety of farm machinery that was sold around the world but also invented the concept of modern toilet paper that we use today.

While it is easy for inventors to extol the significance of their inventions, the success of the improved agricultural machinery developed in this area is substantiated in the industrial record. Several of the manufacturing firms established by local inventors operated for decades, even operating well after the death of the founders, and shipped their products around the world.

PETER DEDERICK, ALBANY

Perpetual Hay Press

By far the most prolific inventor of farming equipment in the Capital District was Peter Kells Dederick, who not only patented an amazing variety of labor-saving machinery but also manufactured and sold it in his own factory on a wide scale for forty years. He is also credited with establishing an important advance in harvesting straw, the concepts of which influenced agricultural machinery for decades.

Dederick was born in Columbia County on February 1, 1838, and educated at the Claverack Academy. Soon afterward, he became interested in hay balers and acquired the patterns of several that were created by others but never fully developed. He developed his first invention, a Parallel Lever Press, in 1854. Although it would later be considered primitive compared to his later improvements, it was a great step forward over others on the market. It was called "the simplest, most compact, easiest working, and powerful hay press in the United States."

In 1860, he established the Albany Agricultural and Machine Works on the west side of Albany near the New York Central Railroad tracks. By that time, his understanding of agricultural machinery was fully developed, and he began patenting hay balers, presses and other equipment by the dozens to be manufactured in his shop.

The most important improvement of the early designs was the use of toggles placed on either end of the machine. The toggles were designed so that their movement caused no friction other than what was applied to the hay being pressed together. Unlike the hay balers of today, Dederick's machine pressed hay together in layers of a few inches each. Bunches of these thin layers of hay were then bound into a bale. Using Dederick's machine, two men and one horse could bale five to eight tons of hay per day. Several independent sources credit his hay press as the most influential of its kind in history, as it led to the beginning of hay baling on farms around the world.

Although the factory met with success in the marketplace, it wasn't until 1872 that Dederick was able to perfect his "perpetual horizontal press." Driven by either hand or horsepower, one man would feed hay into the machine as it moved along while another man bound the hay as it emerged in a compacted form. A reciprocating feeder pushed the hay toward the plunger, forming it into a bale in one swift operation. The operator could change the settings to create almost any size bale, although most were formed in a size weighing one hundred pounds so that they could be easily lifted and stored.

The vast majority of Dederick's patents were improvements to his hay press. New patents were continuously filed to replace those that were expiring, so that he was always covered by patent protection. This was obviously a significant

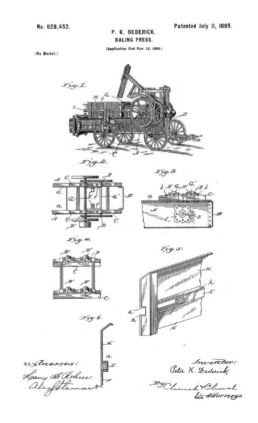

Peter Dederick's "Baling Press."

concern, as manufacturers around the world were tempted to construct and sell the successful invention on their own. Several company advertisements referred to other parties "infringing on our patents."

Besides Dederick's famous hay press, his many other inventions were also manufactured and sold, including farm engines, hoisting machines, tubs, brick machines, dumping carts and horsepowers. The latter subject occupied much of his time, since his early machines were all powered by horses or mules. His horsepower patents included treadmills for one to four horses, a hoisting machine for unloading vessels, a revolving drive wheel arrangement and a "horse-power windlass" designed specifically for his hay press machine.

After forty successful years in the manufacturing business, Dederick retired in 1900 and turned the works over to his sons. More than three decades after his first hay press patent, his perpetual hay press was receiving much attention at the 1904 St. Louis Exposition. Reports from the event called it "the most powerful baling press in the world," and the Albany factory was proclaimed "the baling press headquarters of the world." By that time, Dederick owned over three hundred domestic and foreign patents and was known to have the third largest number of patents awarded to an individual in the United States. He passed away while vacationing in Daytona, Florida, on January 18, 1911.

James Covert, Watervliet

Bolt Harness Snap

Although James Covert was not as prolific an inventor as Peter Dederick, he owned more patents than the vast majority of other inventors and was considered an expert in his chosen field. In fact, his improvements in horse harnesses and snap hooks were so successful that the business he created to manufacture them continued to operate for decades after he passed away.

Covert was born in Seneca County in 1835 and was well educated in the district schools. After graduating school, he worked at a local harness shop. A few years later, he used his new skills in horse equipment manufacture by opening a small factory, but it was not a success and he relocated briefly to Nashville, Tennessee. Upon the outbreak of the Civil War, he returned to New York and settled in Troy. He established the Breast Hold-back Company in 1873 with his brother Madison and brothers Henry and Scudder Wakeman at 210 First Street.

A few years later, the name of the business was changed to the Covert Manufacturing Company to recognize the fact that the company's purpose was to produce Covert's patented inventions. The Covert brothers took full charge upon the departure of the Wakeman brothers, and a new building was erected on the corner of West Street and Central Avenue in Watervliet. Madison Covert severed his ties with the firm in 1893, and James became sole proprietor.

The long list of patents awarded to James Covert beginning in 1878 until his death illustrates the variety of items that he was able to design and manufacture. The snap hooks for which the company was best known consisted of several designs that employed springs to automatically lock the hook into place. One of his several halters, used to lead or tie up a horse, was designed so that it could be easily converted into a bridle, which was used to ride a horse. He also patented such items as a tethering device, fire escape ladder, a trouser stretcher for stretching pant legs, a "girth" for preventing the dislodgement of blankets from horses and a halter tie regulator for keeping animals secure in their stalls. Covert displayed an artistic eye, imparting a decorative quality to many of his inventions, his harnesses in particular. These became known as "Covert's horse and mule jewelry." Fred Covert followed in his father's footsteps and patented over a dozen inventions, mainly for snap hooks.

The company listed an impressive array of snaps, harnesses, rope hooks, lariats, halters, ties and cords for sale, nearly all of which were

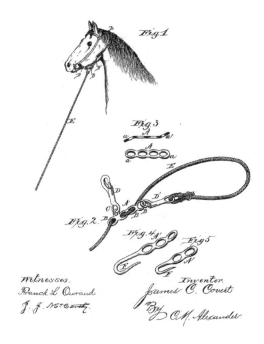

(Model.)

J. C. COVERT.
HARNESS ATTACHMENT.

No. 244,555.   Patented July 19, 1881.

James Covert's "Harness Attachment."

patented. The firm's wrought-iron chains and cables found a market with lumbermen, farmers, dredgers, watercraft builders and car manufacturers. Covert also invented items that catered to tinsmiths and plumbers, such as his patent adjustable soldering irons and coppers. After the turn of the century, Covert's inventions began to change with the times. The Covert Auto Jack was introduced in 1903 for "use on motor vehicles," capable of lifting three thousand pounds. As a side business, Covert established the Dr. Bury Medical Company for the manufacture of lung balsam, catarrh snuff and camphor ointment.

A host of awards and aggressive advertising spread word of Covert's inventions around the world. By 1890, Covert Manufacturing was selling its products to importers based throughout North America and in parts of Europe, Asia and Africa. In 1911, Covert passed away at the age of seventy-six with a portfolio of over fifty patents. The strength of his improved harnesses, hooks and other inventions enabled Covert Manufacturing to become one of the few nineteenth-century manufacturers in the Capital District to survive the Great Depression and beyond.

LEWIS ASPINWALL, ALBANY

Potato Planters and Diggers

Now an outmoded technology, the refinement of potato planters and diggers in the late 1800s was a tremendous aid to farmers across the country. Potatoes became an important staple crop because they were high in calories compared to other foods, were easy to grow and could be stored for relatively long periods. However, planting and harvesting potatoes by hand was backbreaking labor that involved harrowing, plowing and rolling the ground to get an effective crop yield.

Some of the most effective and popular potato-growing machinery in America was developed by Lewis Augustus Aspinwall, who was born on October 14, 1842, in Hastings, Westchester County, and educated at the Albany Academy. His father was a bell foundryman, but at a young age, Aspinwall displayed an interest in farming pursuits. When he was twelve years old, he invented an implement for drilling garden seed that was used on the family farm for many years.

After finishing school, he moved to Albany and began to develop an idea for a potato planter. The first versions were flawed, but he continued to refine the design over a period of twenty years. In the meantime, he invented the first successful corn husker, able to husk at the rate of one bushel per minute. It was so effective that he was able to sell the patent for $20,000. He used the money to travel to Europe and conduct experiments with a variety of potato planters and diggers throughout the continent. In 1874 and 1878, he took out patents in Great Britain for an improved potato planter, which he referenced in an American patent filed a few years later.

When Aspinwall returned to America, he settled in the Albany suburb of Loudonville and resumed patenting a variety of farming implements. His extensive experiments in Europe gave him a thorough understanding of how the current potato machines functioned and the problems associated with the designs. Many of his patent letters describe the variety of flaws in the machinery on the market and what he did to correct them.

His most famous patent was his fully automatic potato planter. It was the first patented planter to open the furrow, drop the seeds (or "eyes") at a set distance apart and close the furrow, all in one operation. Another important machine was his two-row planter, which allowed one man and a team of horses to plant crops twice as fast as the standard single-row planters. The hopper, or seed holder, enabled a farmer to plant seeds for half a mile at a time. His crop sprayer included attachments that could be used for all purposes, including ground crops and orchards. One driver was able to spray up to twenty acres per day.

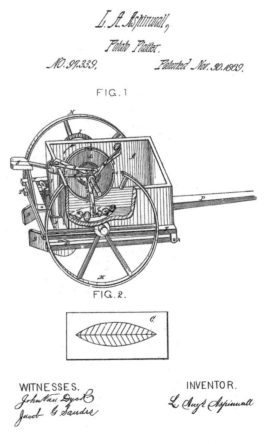

Lewis Aspinwall's "Improvement in Machine for Planting Potatoes."

Aspinwall's potato sorter could sort up to one thousand bushels per day into three sizes and was mainly used by commercial growers.

After Aspinwall patented several dozen inventions in Albany County, a capitalist named C.W. Briggs of Chicago offered to invest in a factory to produce his machinery. Aspinwall decided to relocate to Three Rivers, Michigan, in 1884 to establish the Aspinwall Manufacturing Company. Within a few years, the firm was shipping goods to markets all over the country and employed thirty men. By that time, Aspinwall was advertising sprayers, cutters, diggers, churns, weeders and lawn swings, claiming that his company was "the only concern in the world making a complete line of potato machinery."

Despite the remarkable improvements made by Aspinwall in farm machinery, the tide of progress finally caught up with him, and in 1925 his company was purchased by the McKenzie Manufacturing Company. Aspinwall apparently enjoyed good health, as he went to work for McKenzie at the age of eighty-three, but he passed away five years later on November 5, 1930. The patents he filed in Albany are considered to be among the most effective and popular potato machine improvements in history, and they relieved many farmers of the drudgery of growing potatoes by hand.

JOHN GRISWOLD, TROY

Wire Straightener

Some products seem so simple that they could not possibly be improved upon, but John Wool Griswold's modification of baling wire created a demand from farmers that even he could not have imagined. In addition to the Troy factory, several companies were established halfway across the country just to manufacture his bale and fencing wire.

Griswold was born on August 30, 1850, in Troy, nephew of famous Civil War general John Wool and the son of John Augustus Griswold. The elder Griswold owned a large steel foundry in Troy that purchased the domestic rights to the English patents of the Bessemer steel-making process. Although Griswold Sr. was elected mayor of Troy in 1855, he is best known as the man who helped finance the Union ironclad warship *Monitor* during the Civil War (see the chapter "Men of Steel").

The younger Griswold attended the Troy Academy and Williams College but left before he completed his degree. Following the death of his father, he became superintendent of the Bessemer Steel Works. Desiring to operate his own business, in 1879 he and his brother Frank established the Griswold Wire Works on the banks of the Hudson River near Congress Street. The company was created on the strength of a wire-straightening process that Griswold perfected. Wire was placed on a rotary support and fed through an annealing furnace. Moving rolls drew the wire forward and deposited it on a table, where it was cut into suitable lengths by an automatic knife. As the wire was drawn through the furnace, a combination of heat and tension caused it to become permanently straightened. The type of wire made in this process was used primarily for fencing.

Griswold also patented a machine for producing bale tie wire. The tie was manufactured with a loop at one end. After the band was wrapped around the bale of hay, the end was passed through a V-shaped saddle. When the wire was tightened, it jammed against the angle of the saddle as well as being compressed into the eye loop, which locked the wire securely in place.

The Griswold Wire Works was a substantial brick building three stories high. By 1890, the company employed 150 men and was producing 3,500 tons of wire per year. The brothers also manufactured twenty thousand kegs of wire nails up to eight inches long using nineteen patent nail machines.

Both Griswold and his brother were prodigious inventors with dozens of patents awarded, mainly during the 1880s and 1890s. Fence posts, bale ties, barbed-wire fencing, wire straightening and wire bending machines were the most common, but others included a fire screen, pneumatic tire and a fountain pen holder. One machine was patented to create the eye hooks noted on the hay bale wire above, while another machine was patented for applying the hooks to the wire.

In 1896, Griswold partnered with William Dillon of Rock Falls, Illinois, to form the Dillon-Griswold Wire Company. The firm was almost identical to the one in Troy, as it manufactured the barbed wire and bale ties that Griswold patented over the years (but on a larger scale, producing 35,000 tons of wire and 315,000 kegs of wire nails annually). Upon Griswold's death, Dillon purchased all of the stock in the company and formed the Northwestern Steel and Wire Company. Another firm called the Griswold Wire Company was established in Braddock, Pennsylvania, which manufactured his patent steel loop and hook bale ties.

John Griswold took an active interest in his hometown, serving as a trustee for the Troy Savings Bank, the Troy Orphan Asylum, the Samaritan Hospital and the Troy Club. While on a business trip to Chicago with his wife, he passed away unexpectedly of heart disease on January 2, 1902. His brother Frank decided to move to Egypt, but the Troy factory continued to operate for another decade. The buildings have since been torn down, and only a few foundation ruins remain of this once prosperous business.

GEORGE WESTINGHOUSE SR., SCHENECTADY

Agricultural Machines

There are two men with the name of George Westinghouse in this book, a father and his son. The son is one of the most famous inventors of all time and owned one of railroading's most famous patents. Although the son's invention completely overshadows those of his father, George Westinghouse Sr. was a gifted inventor in his own right, patenting several inventions that found success in the marketplace.

Westinghouse was born in Pownal, Vermont, on March 20, 1809. He grew up on a large farm where he developed a gift for building labor-saving devices for harvesting crops. Upon coming of age, he sought new opportunities by heading west as far as Ohio. However, conditions there were still unsettled, so he returned to northeastern New York and settled in Central Bridge, Schoharie County. He established a small shop for building farm machinery but decided that prospects for success would be more promising elsewhere. Therefore, in 1856, he moved his large family to Schenectady and established the Schenectady Agricultural Works under the firm name G. Westinghouse Company.

Over the next ten years, Westinghouse was awarded thirty patents for agricultural implements that were constructed and sold in his factory. It was said that each invention was worked out in every detail and with such completeness that a skilled mechanic could construct any of the machines from the patent letters. One of his biggest sellers was an improved grain separator that consisted of two carriers connected to a thresher into which the grain was fed. By the time the grain passed over the two vibrating seed carriers, which moved in opposite directions, the grain seeds were effectively separated from the straw. Other agricultural machines included an improved hay baler, soil harrower, grain reaper and an endless-chain horsepower device.

The G. Westinghouse Company (later renamed the Westinghouse Farm Machinery Company) grew in size and manufactured thousands of mill machines, small steam engines and Westinghouse's patented agricultural machines. The factory was situated near the General Electric campus convenient to both the Erie Canal and the New York Central Railroad. The primary production center was a brick building three stories high measuring three hundred feet by five hundred feet, surrounded by a foundry, blacksmith shop and warehouses. Up to two hundred men were employed who produced 300 threshers, 150 steam engines and hundreds of other farming implements annually.

Beyond the increase in productivity that his machinery provided to farmers, Westinghouse's greatest contribution to society was providing a fully equipped shop to his sons for experimentation and real-time educational experiences. It was at the Westinghouse Company's shop that George Jr. conceived and built his first inventions, which paved the way for the prodigious output to follow.

Westinghouse retired from active employment in his business in 1870, but operations were carried on by two of his sons, both of whom also

G. WESTINGHOUSE.

Grain Separator.

No. 27,941.   Patented April 17, 1860.

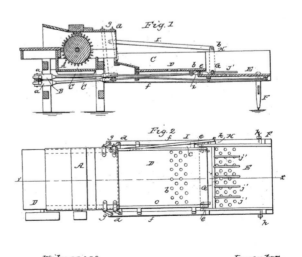

George
Westinghouse
Sr.'s "Grain
Separator."

patented several agricultural machines. He relocated to Philadelphia to be close to George Jr., who had established the Westinghouse Air Brake Company during the previous year and was rapidly accumulating fame and fortune. In retirement, he remained interested in his company, directing its activities from afar until 1884, when he passed away at his son's home. The Westinghouse Company continued to operate for several more decades but was shut down in 1921, as no further improvements were being made to its products. The land was purchased by General Electric to accommodate its expansion, and no trace of the business exists today.

SETH WHEELER, ALBANY

Farm Machinery and Perforated Paper

One of Albany's most famous inventions came from one of the city's most prolific inventors. He was also one of the few inventors to find success in two entirely different careers: one in manufacturing agricultural implements and the other in the paper industry.

Seth Wheeler was born in Chatham, New York, on May 18, 1838. After receiving an education at Albany Academy, he joined his father Alonzo in a factory that made farm machinery and tools. It was first established in Chatham by Alonzo and his brother William but was moved to Albany in 1849. Seth became a partner in the firm when Alonzo passed away the following year. Reorganized as the New York State Agricultural Works under the partnership of Wheeler, Melick and Company, it became a leading farm machinery manufacturer with 125 employees and $500,000 in annual sales.

Part of the firm's success came from Seth Wheeler's new machinery patents. An advertisement in the *Cultivator* boasted the success of "Wheeler's Patent Railway Chain Horse Powers, Overshot Thresher and Separator, Straw and Stalk Cutters, and Clover Hullers." Thousands of his overshot threshers and separators were sold around the country, amounting to four times as many as the next highest-selling brand. It was called "one of the best agricultural machines ever invented, and that it is appreciated by the farming interest is evidenced by the fact that it has been sold in nearly every state in the Union, including California and Oregon."

His patent "Combined Thresher and Winnower" machine was developed soon after he became a partner and was able to thresh and clean up to two hundred bushels of wheat or four hundred bushels of oats per day using two horses. A separate rye threshing machine accepted rye into a long cylinder, which fed the straw between two corrugated surfaces to remove the grain. The threshed straw was then deposited in neat bundles by an endless apron.

Wheeler took particular interest in horsepower machines, of which he had several patents. Some historians believe that he manufactured the first endless chain horsepower of single gear. His improved revolving horsepowers, employing horses that would turn a power wheel by walking in a circle, were designed to take the weight of the wheel on the pulleys rather than on the central journal. This reduced the friction normally found between the wheel and the frame, allowing a horse to work longer with less strain.

The other type of horsepower involved a treadmill design. Large, inclined boxes were constructed to hold one or more horses. As the animals walked forward, the platform moved a pulley system that powered a variety of machines. Smaller machines known as "pony power" were developed to be run by a calf or pony to perform such duties as churning dairy machines or pumping water. Dog lovers will likely cringe at the thought of his "dog power" machine, although it was advised that "a sheep of a large breed is much better than a dog for working this power, as the work is less irksome to the sheep." Wheeler's "Iron King" horsepower machine, which could accommodate up to ten horses, won more premiums at national, state and county fairs than any other machine in use. The firm sold thousands of machines each year.

Although his agricultural machine manufacturing company was one of the most successful in the area, Wheeler's inventive mind was constantly looking for solutions to common problems. One day it occurred to him that the practice of bundling various types of paper was laborious and inefficient. The process of organizing, counting and stacking paper could be eliminated by utilizing rolls of paper that contained regularly spaced perforations. As a side project, he set about designing machinery and accessories for manufacturing perforated paper.

At first, he confined his inspiration to wrapping paper. Wheeler's "Improvement in Wrapping Papers" patent was awarded on July 20, 1871, and was the precursor to dozens of perforated paper and paper machine patents. He was so excited about this simple yet groundbreaking idea that the following year he resigned from the New York State Agricultural Works to organize the Rolled Wrapping Paper Company at 318 Broadway in Albany. This company was not able to make a profit, but he was undeterred. After making several improvements to his machinery and applying the concept to other uses, he formed the Albany Perforated Wrapping Paper Company in 1877.

One of the uses he envisioned for his perforated paper was bathroom tissue. Although rolled toilet paper was currently available, Wheeler's inventions of perforated paper, a cardboard tube to serve as the base, a rolled paper holder and the machines to manufacture these articles all but guaranteed the success of his new company. Known in the trade as "APW Paper," it grew rapidly as Wheeler's idea for perforated paper spread around the world. Plants and offices were eventually established in New York City, Chicago, Boston, San Francisco, London, Berlin, Paris, Cologne and Switzerland. Although the most obvious and widely used forms of Wheeler's perforated design was and still is toilet paper, a wide variety of papers was manufactured and sold. His patent medicated paper was made for "sufferers from hemorrhoids, affording a means of securing for chronic cases that regular, persistent treatment without which the advice of the ablest physicians fail to relieve." He also patented an "anti-rust" paper for "bright goods," which provided the "perfect protection from dampness."

The Albany location on Broadway continued to be the main manufacturing plant and offices for the company. The buildings measured two hundred feet by three hundred feet and occupied nearly three square acres of floor space. By 1915, production amounted to two million pounds of paper products per month from machines that were nearly all patented by Wheeler. The great demand for kitchen and restroom papers persuaded him to abandon most other products and concentrate on toilet paper and paper towels. The *Albany Guide Book* boasted that the "APW Paper company's products are demanded by every hotel, restaurant, home, office, railroad train, and steamboat in the world and are sold through branch offices covering the civilized globe."

Wheeler was awarded almost one hundred domestic and foreign patents, about half relating to his perforated paper idea. Other inventions included an ore washer, an improved paper box, an improvement in barrel heads, a permutation lock, improved pulleys and a saw machine. He also established the Wheeler Rent and Power Company and served as its president, was vice-president of the Cheney Piano Action Company of Castleton and was president of the Albany County Savings Bank. His sons Edgar, William and Seth Jr. all served as officers in the APW Paper Company. He passed away at his home on Lark Street on May 22, 1925, at the age of eighty-eight.

HAULING THE WORLD

The second half of Schenectady's slogan, "The City That Lights and Hauls the World," referred to the mammoth plant of the Schenectady Locomotive Works. First formed by a group of locals in 1848, the company floundered at first with a locomotive product that was too large for the rails of the time. However, in 1854, the company was given a new lease on life and began manufacturing the types of locomotives that the market demanded.

Over the following decades, building after building was added until the plant occupied more than twenty acres of land on the northeast side of Schenectady, straddling the Erie Canal. In 1869, the Schenectady-built locomotive Jupiter conveyed Governor Stanford and his party from Sacramento, California, to Ogden, Utah, for the golden spike ceremony connecting the Union Pacific and Central Pacific Railroads.

Schenectady Locomotive experienced a long period of growth during the latter half of the nineteenth century, thanks in part to the efforts of inventor Albert Pitkin. Until he arrived in 1882, the company concentrated on producing small locomotives with only eight wheels (four leading wheels and four driving wheels). Pitkin was a proponent of the larger and faster locomotives that were needed to handle the rapidly growing freight and passenger business. His efforts in designing the first successful cross-compound locomotive, described later, were only a small part of his contribution to the prosperity of the company.

By 1901, the Schenectady Locomotive Works was one of the largest locomotive manufacturers in the country. In that year, it merged with seven others to become the American Locomotive Company, better known as

The American Locomotive Company inspired several inventors, such as Francis Cole and Albert Pitkin, to develop important innovations in railroad technology. *Courtesy of the Efner City History Center.*

"Alco." Dozens of innovations were made by Alco engineers in the years that followed. Chief Engineer Francis Cole perfected a superheating system that provided more power to a locomotive's driving wheels than ever before. In addition to implementing Cole's superheater to many of its locomotives, Alco built some of the first "articulated" locomotives, with two sets of driving wheels for greater traction. Perhaps its most famous locomotive was the "Big Boy," one of the largest steam engines ever built. Designed specifically for the Union Pacific's mountain lines in Utah and Wyoming, it was able to produce over six thousand horsepower and pull a train one mile long.

Alco ultimately built seventy-five thousand steam engines, more than any other company except Baldwin. Through most of its history, the company was the second-largest employer in Schenectady (after General Electric), with some 2,500 employees. Although it diversified into diesel engines beginning in 1924, it could not compete in the long term with General Motors and General Electric. Alco finally closed its Schenectady plant in 1969.

The engineers and designers of Schenectady Locomotive were not the only inventors to affect the transportation industry. James McElroy of Albany, one of the area's most prolific inventors, designed a host of railroad-related innovations that made their way into manufacturing processes around the country. Although George Westinghouse moved out of the area soon after his famous invention was patented, he conceived the idea for what could arguably be called the most important railroad improvement in history here in the Capital District. Barnabas Langdon of Troy developed a new type of ferryboat that would today be considered outlandish at best but was adopted in several parts of the country and used for twenty years.

Barnabas Langdon, Troy

Horse-Powered Ferry

In an age when bridges spanning large rivers were scarce, ferryboats were an important part of the Capital District's transportation system. For many years, they were the only method of crossing the area's largest rivers, particularly the Mohawk and the Hudson. The first ferry across the Hudson, dating back to 1642, was a primitive scow propelled by a man pushing down on a long pole. Other ferries were modified rowboats or sailboats.

Although steamboats were rising in popularity at the time, they typically cost as much as $30,000 each. A more economical horse-powered ferryboat that cost about $12,000 was developed as an alternative. The first such boat made its debut in New York City in 1814, featuring horses that walked in circles to move a central post. However, the circular walkway took up a lot of space on the cramped deck, and the incessant walking in circles was exhausting to the horses.

A local inventor named Barnabas Langdon achieved some fame around the country for his unique modification to horse ferries. He built a rotating turntable slightly below the surface of the deck on which the horses would walk, which drove the treadmill backward. This was not only healthier for the horses but also freed up a great deal of room on the deck. His design was quickly recognized for its efficiency, reliability and low cost. For more than twenty years, the horizontal tread wheel ferry was the most common type of horse boat, especially in the New England and mid-Atlantic states. Other inventors used the idea to develop land-based treadmill arrangements to power farm machinery.

Langdon held at least nine patents, making him one of the area's most prolific inventors of the early 1800s. Half related to different modes of propelling boats, while the others were for a grain grinder, a stave joiner, a lathe machine and several planing machines. The *Troy Budget* noted in 1826 that Langdon had invented a new type of steamboat consisting of "two boats, three hundred feet long, and decked over the whole length, in the shape and mould very much like the Indian bark canoe." The original papers and models of his patents were all destroyed in the Patent Office fire of 1836, but a few were subsequently replaced, including his famous treadmill horse boat.

As the country became more industrialized during and after the Civil War, the need for ferryboats began to wane. Long bridges began to cross major rivers, while the rapid expansion of railroads caused many people to travel by rail rather than on foot or horseback. The advent of the internal

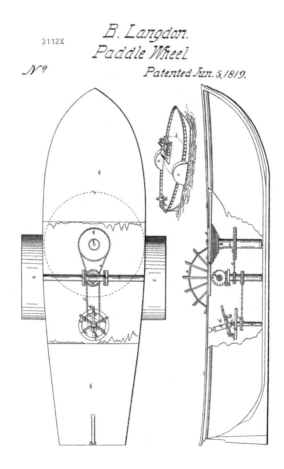

Barnabus Langdon's "Propelling Boats by Horsepower."

combustion engine, which doomed even the steam engine to obsolescence, finally caused the horse ferryboat to disappear altogether.

In 1983, underwater archaeologists sponsored by the Champlain Maritime Society and the Vermont Division for Historic Preservation conducted a study of Lake Champlain to locate and document its shipwrecks. One shipwreck drew particular attention—a boat that contained a pair of paddlewheels but had no boiler or steam engine. In their report to state officials, the archaeologists suspected that they had found a rare example of the famous treadmill horse ferries. While photographing the vessel, they discovered fragments of a horse collar, leather harness straps and broken horseshoes. They also found a spot on the hull where one of the planks was missing, and the rudder was lying near the bow of the boat about sixty feet from its normal location at the rear. The gears were heavily worn down, and the hull was only half an inch thick in some places. These indications led the team to believe that the boat had been intentionally sunk after many years of hard service.

Francis Cole, Schenectady

Locomotive Superheater

Several gifted employees of the Schenectady Locomotive Works devised dozens, if not hundreds, of improvements in railroad technology that affected rail transportation around the country. One of the most important technological leaps was perfected by Francis J. Cole, who was born in England in 1856. After immigrating to America with his family, he began a distinguished career in locomotive design at the West Shore Railroad, the Baltimore and Ohio Railroad and the Rogers Locomotive Works in Passaic, New Jersey. When the American Locomotive Company (Alco) was formed in 1901, he decided to join the new firm and relocated to the Schenectady plant, where he became chief engineer.

During his time at Alco, Cole developed a variety of innovations for locomotives that dramatically increased their power while lowering their overall weight to achieve maximum efficiency. One became known as the Cole Trailing Truck, which was a set of wheels added to the back of the engine that did not need the usual outside frames. This improvement removed two tons of weight from the back of the engine and became the standard configuration for more than a decade. Cole also devised a series of

"Cole Ratios" in 1914 for measuring locomotive performance. For example, total machine efficiency was derived by dividing the engine weight by the grate area.

Alco's fifty-thousandth locomotive was personally designed by Cole as a demonstration model that set new records in locomotive performance and low weight. It was the first Pacific-class engine to have a cylinder bore of twenty-seven inches and a boiler that was large enough to supply the cylinders with enough superheated steam for continuous operation. His efforts were hampered by the fact that automatic firebox stokers had not been perfected enough for reliable use, so the engine was hand fired. However, it was still able to generate more horsepower than any other engine of its kind. This locomotive became the inspiration for Pennsylvania Railroad's class K4

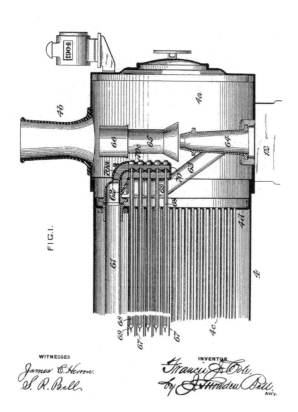

No. 765,307.

PATENTED JULY 19, 1904.

F. J. COLE.
STEAM BOILER SUPERHEATER.
APPLICATION FILED APR. 21, 1904.

3 SHEETS—SHEET 1.

FIG. I.

WITNESSES
James C. Herron.
S. R. Bell.

INVENTOR
Francis J. Cole,
by J. Herndon Bell,
Att'y.

Francis Cole's "Steam Boiler Superheater."

Pacific and the Chesapeake and Ohio's class F-16 Pacific, two of the most popular and acclaimed steam locomotives.

Of the several dozen patents awarded to Cole over his career, perhaps the most important series were for his locomotive superheaters. In 1904, he began developing an arrangement that carried hot gases through long pipes and widened tubes, known as flues. These tubes doubled back on themselves so that the gases could not only convert water to steam in the usual manner but then "superheat" the steam that had just been created as well. This superheated steam provided greater power while using about 10 to 20 percent less coal and water.

The Cole Superheater (also called the Alco Superheater, since Cole assigned the invention to his employer) enjoyed widespread use and was installed on thousands of locomotives. Dozens of other inventions were developed by Cole during his years at Alco, such as a valve stem guide, tender vestibule, drifting valve, electric locomotive, crank shaft, improved steam pipes and a variety of locomotive engines. He is considered to be one of the most brilliant and gifted engineers in the history of American Locomotive, providing templates and inspiration for a variety of popular Atlantic-, Pacific- and Britannia-class steam locomotives. He passed away in Pasadena, California, on January 11, 1923.

ALBERT PITKIN, SCHENECTADY

Compound Engine

The remarkable success of the Schenectady Locomotive Works was due in large part to the efforts of Albert Johnson Pitkin, who acted as a manager in various capacities for over twenty years. During his tenure, the capacity of the plant increased from 185 light locomotives per year to almost 1,000 locomotives of both light and heavy designs.

Pitkin was born on March 22, 1854, in Northampton, Ohio, to a Presbyterian minister and his wife, the latter passing away when Pitkin was just nine years old. He trained as a machinist in the stationary engine works of the Webster, Camp and Lane Machine Company in Akron and then spent a year in the locomotive repair shops of the Akron and Columbus Railway. However, his most valuable vocational experience came from his time at the Baldwin Locomotive Works, the largest manufacturer of locomotives in the United States.

Albert Pitkin (1854–1905).
Courtesy of the Efner City History Center.

He made his final career move in 1882 by accepting the position of mechanical engineer at the Schenectady Locomotive Works. Pitkin's hard work and outgoing personality made him a standout in the engineering department, and he soon became superintendent at the young age of thirty. Upon the death of Edward Ellis, he was made vice-president and general manager, taking charge of sales and commercial management while retaining his duties in the other departments.

His greatest contribution to locomotive technology was his refinement of compound engines. Standard locomotive engines suffered from inefficiencies when the temperature of the steam dropped as it expanded in the cylinder. In a compound engine, steam is released into a high-pressure cylinder and then into a low-pressure cylinder. Since the steam is able to expand across multiple cylinders of varying pressure, there is less of a drop in heat, which in turn equates to a more efficient locomotive.

Pitkin introduced a variety of improvements to compound engines, which until that time were considered by many to be too complicated to justify. In his first design, patented in 1892, Pitkin had perfected his intercepting valve arrangement, which was the hallmark of his compound engine improvement. The stem of the valve was connected by levers to an index in the cab so that the engineer could easily see its position. After the engine was started in the usual way, a small pipe from the boiler through a reducing valve supplied steam to the low-pressure cylinder at a reduced pressure. When enough pressure had accumulated in the receiver, the intercepting valve was forced into position for becoming compound. Locomotives built with the Pitkin Compound, as the system became known, used 18 percent less coal than a "simple" engine.

A more flexible and successful design was patented by Pitkin four years later. The arrangement of valves enabled the engine to be started as either compound or simple and could be changed at any time from compound to simple and back again by the engineer. This was useful if the compound mechanisms malfunctioned, in which case the engine could be operated as

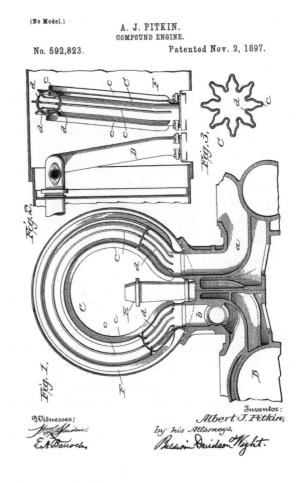

(No Model.)

A. J. PITKIN.
COMPOUND ENGINE.

No. 592,823.

Patented Nov. 2, 1897.

Witnesses:

Inventor:
Albert J. Pitkin,
by his Attorneys,

Albert Pitkin's "Compound Engine."

a simple engine until repairs could be made. The engineer would also desire to turn off compounding when more power was needed to climb steep gradients under heavy load.

Four of Pitkin's dozen patents concerned his compound locomotives. Others included a lighter railroad car truck design, an improved throttle valve arrangement and a locomotive that utilized large trailing wheels as well as a mechanism for shifting weight from the driving wheels to the trailing wheels. He also patented a steam-propelled car in which the boiler and engine were located at one end of the car while passenger seats occupied the other end.

Pitkin was named president of Alco upon the death of Samuel Callaway in 1904. However, it was said that his working life had been "too absorbing and too anxious," and he passed away only a year later on November 16, 1905. Of the relatively few innovative design modifications to compound engines, Pitkin's was one of the most widely accepted. Approximately three thousand non-articulated compound locomotives were built by the time Pitkin passed away, thanks in part to his unique intercepting valve and cylinder arrangement.

JAMES MCELROY, ALBANY

Car Heating Systems

The accomplishments of some inventors are somewhat staggering. It is exceedingly rare for an individual to make a living by being an inventor and rarer still for him to market his inventions in a successful manner over a number of years. James McElroy not only achieved these lofty goals with dozens of patents but became a prominent and influential member of society as well.

McElroy was born on November 25, 1852, in Greenfield, Ohio, and attended South Salem College and Dartmouth University. Upon graduating, he served as principal of the Indiana Institute of the Blind for four years and superintendent of the Michigan Institution of the Blind for seven years. During his time in these institutions, he began to experiment with mathematics, physics, chemistry and electricity.

In 1887, after patenting a few inventions relating to railroad car heating systems, he moved to Albany and formed the McElroy Car Heating Company. The business was a success, and two years later it was merged with the Sewell Car Heating Company to become the Consolidated Car-Heating

Company (CCHC). Two of the original stockholders of the firm were James Roosevelt, father of Franklin D. Roosevelt, and author James Fenimore Cooper. In 1890, George Westinghouse joined the board of directors and acquired $400,000 worth of CCHC stock. A building was erected on Pearl Street in 1893 to house the growing company, followed by a second building in 1906 and a third in 1914. By the turn of the century, it was already the largest manufacturer of electric heaters in the country.

McElroy began submitting a deluge of patents after the formation of CCHC, sometimes averaging more than two a month. Many of his patents were complex in nature, spanning twenty or more pages, when most patents consisted of no more than two written pages and a drawing. Adhering to his original premise, the vast majority were for railroad car heating systems powered by steam, hot water, fire and electricity. Many were manufactured

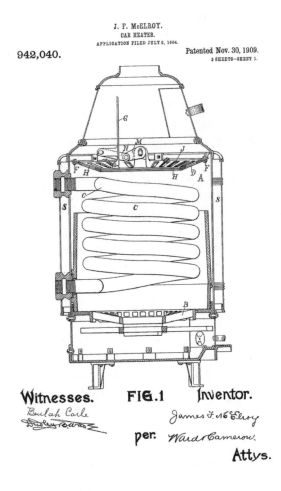

J. F. McELROY.
CAR HEATER.
APPLICATION FILED JULY 5, 1904.

942,040.

Patented Nov. 30, 1909.
3 SHEETS—SHEET 1.

Witnesses.   **FIG.1**   **Inventor.**

Beulah Carle

James F. McElroy

per. Ward Cameron.

Attys.

James McElroy's
"Car Heater."

and sold to railroads around the country. For example, CCHC contracted with the New York Central Railroad to install McElroy's steam heating system in its entire fleet of passenger cars. McElroy was particularly influential in developing heating systems for trolleys, with his inventions becoming adopted by many trolley lines.

A wide variety of other patents were awarded for items such as safety switch panels, universal joints, hot water heaters, ventilators and thermostats. McElroy's passenger doors were particularly successful and consisted of manual folding or sliding doors, compressed air-powered doors with push-button remote control and pneumatic car step–operated doors. In 1909, the country's first subway car with side doors was put into operation in New York City on the Interborough Rapid Transit Company. The doors were positioned four feet from the ends of each car and operated with McElroy's patented pneumatic lever system.

With over three hundred patents to his name, McElroy would be considered unique for that fact alone. However, he also held a number of prominent positions in the community and somehow found time for a variety of causes. He served as a director in the Albany Exchange Savings Bank, Albany Mutual Insurance Company, the United Traction Company, the Hudson Valley Electric Railroad and the Albany Orphan Society, as well as many clubs and associations. The Consolidated Car-Heating Company operated until 1958, when it exited the transportation business and transformed into CMP Industries to manufacture dental equipment. McElroy passed away on February 10, 1915, as one of the Capital District's most talented and prolific inventors.

GEORGE WESTINGHOUSE JR., SCHENECTADY

Railroad Air Brake

The air brake of George Westinghouse Jr. is arguably the most famous invention to come from the Capital District. It almost single-handedly permitted the astounding growth of railroads beginning in 1870. A short time after it was adopted by railroads nationwide, it was written that "with his air-brake, Westinghouse has saved more lives than Napoleon lost in all of his battles." Although the vast majority of his three hundred patents were awarded after he moved from the area, his air brake was first conceived in Schenectady, and the first patent for it was filed in that city.

George Westinghouse Jr.
(1846–1914) as a young
man. *Courtesy of the Library
of Congress.*

Westinghouse was born on October 6, 1846, in Central Bridge, a short distance west of Schenectady. He and his brothers were encouraged from an early age by their father to experiment and invent new devices. When the family moved to Schenectady to enlarge the business, George spent most of his time working and tinkering in his father's large and well-equipped machine shop. Each of the five brothers was challenged to build an engine of original pattern before he turned sixteen. George decided to take on the difficult project of constructing a rotary engine. Although it was never built or marketed commercially, he took out a patent for the engine and continued to tinker with it for the rest of his life.

The Civil War broke out when Westinghouse was fifteen years old. His father would not let him join the army with his brothers at that time, but two years later he enlisted in the Twelfth New York Infantry and served until the war ended. When he returned home, his parents asked that he attend Union College, but he was only able to last three months before quitting and returning to his father's shop. His restless mind could not bear to sit in a classroom for any length of time.

His first successful invention was conceived on his way home one night from Albany. His train was forced to stop for several hours while a freight car ahead was being placed back on the tracks after derailing. Westinghouse watched as the crew jacked the car back on the tracks inch by inch and marveled at the crudeness of their methods. Back at his father's shop, he devised a car rerailer that essentially worked by clamping a section of rail to the track next to the derailed car wheel and using the locomotive to haul the car back on the track. His father did not believe the railroads would purchase the invention and refused to fund it. However, Westinghouse was undeterred and used what little savings he had to have his rerailer manufactured in Troy. A short time later, he invented a reversible steel frog to be used at the intersection of railroad tracks.

The idea for his greatest invention occurred to him a year later on one of his daily trips from Schenectady to the foundry in Troy where his rerailers were being made. His train was held up by a bad wreck in which two freight trains collided head-on with each other on a section of straight track. The engineers saw the impending collision but could not stop the trains in time.

Stopping a train at that time was a slow and dangerous process. The engineer could only apply brakes to the locomotive, which by itself could not stop a train of any sizeable length. Each car, therefore, was equipped with a hand brake. When the train had to be stopped, the engineer would signal the brakemen, who would climb from car to car, turning each hand brake to a stop position. This prevented railroads from operating at high speeds or with long trains.

As Westinghouse stood looking at the two wrecked freight trains, he decided that there had to be a better way to stop a train. Several ideas for an automatic brake came to him over the course of the next few months, from brakes attached to couplers to brakes powered by steam. Two perplexing obstacles stood in his way: how to provide enough power to operate the brakes for the length of a train, and how to devise a system that would apply braking simultaneously to all cars. Fate again stepped in for the answer. During one hot August day working at his father's shop, a young girl appeared at the door selling magazines. Westinghouse purchased a subscription to *Living Age*, and in the first delivery there was an article about drills powered by compressed air that were used to build the Mount Cenis Tunnel. A sudden inspiration gave him the breakthrough he was looking for. He threw down the magazine and began sketching plans for the world's first air brake.

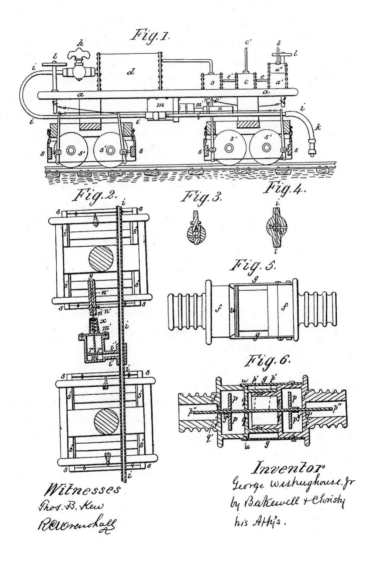

G. WESTINGHOUSE, JR

STEAM POWER BRAKE

NO. 88,929.

PATENTED APR. 13, 1869

George Westinghouse Jr.'s "Improvement in Steam Power Brake Devices."

Although he quickly patented his invention, the most difficult task was before him. Many thousands of inventions have been devised that were never used because their makers could not induce others to purchase them. At that time, dozens of proposals for an improved braking system were being sent to railroad managers. It was difficult for them to choose which one would be most effective without spending thousands of dollars in development and testing.

When no one in Schenectady would give Westinghouse the required funding, he went to Pittsburgh and met a man named Ralph Bagley who owned a foundry and agreed to manufacture the first air brake for testing. The initial trials successfully proved that his system worked, and word of Westinghouse's air brake began to spread among railroad executives. By 1876, almost 40 percent of all domestic trains were equipped with Westinghouse's air brake. He continued to modify and perfect his system over the years with a total of twenty patents, until it was adopted by almost every railroad in the country and around the world.

Westinghouse remained in Pennsylvania as the rest of his remarkable career unfolded. From his air brake he turned to electricity and advocated for alternating current over direct current, which was safer but could not be transmitted more than a short distance. He formed the Westinghouse Electrical Company and became the chief rival of Thomas Edison and General Electric. He obtained the exclusive rights to Nikola Tesla's patents for a polyphase system of alternating current while submitting hundreds of his own patents. By 1900, Westinghouse's companies were valued at $120 million and employed fifty thousand workers. The financial panic of 1907 caused him to lose millions of dollars as well as control of his business empire, but when he died on March 12, 1914, he still possessed a respectable fortune.

The city of Schenectady holds a high place in the world of patented inventions, mainly thanks to the American Locomotive Company and General Electric, but since Westinghouse moved out of the area at a young age, most of his patents do not carry Schenectady's name on them. It is a small consolation, however, that his first inventions were conceived and patented in Schenectady, including his famous and historic air brake.

HEATING THE WORLD

For more than a century, the heating and cooking stove industry was one of the largest in the Capital District, and the collective manufactured output of stoves was among the highest in the world. Albany and Troy were vitally important in the early development of the domestic stove industry due to both the huge manufacturing firms that were established in these cities as well as the inventors who improved the designs of the earliest stoves.

The American stove industry received its first breakthrough from Benjamin Franklin, who developed an iron fireplace-stove combination that jutted out into the room to provide heat from three sides rather than the traditional one-sided fireplace. The next innovations were the box stove, later used mainly for heating large spaces, and the cooking stove, essentially a box stove containing an oven.

Several businessmen established stove factories in Albany beginning about 1810, although for the first few years the castings were made in the blast furnaces of New Jersey and shipped to Albany for assembly. Before long, the first foundries were established, small at first but growing in size every year. By 1850, both Albany and Troy contained several of the world's largest stove foundries and dozens of smaller ones.

Union College president Eliphalet Nott conceived the earliest and most famous stove in the region when he developed the first anthracite coal–burning stove. Joel Rathbone of Albany came to prominence soon after with improved stoves of his own. After assembling stoves cast by others for a few years, he erected a cupola furnace in 1838, which is believed to be the first in the country designed for the sole purpose of producing stove castings. His stoves found an immediate market, and the physical plant of the Rathbone Stove Works grew until it covered two acres of land. In 1860, over thirty-five thousand stoves were shipped from Rathbone's foundry alone.

The extent of manufacturing in the two cities is apparent from the list of over three hundred stove manufacturers in Albany and Troy from 1810 to 1930. The Capital District was not only the single largest stove producer in the country, but it was also considered the "Stove Design Capital of the World," as a host of area inventors patented new designs as well as groundbreaking improvements. Albany's Dennis Littlefield patented the Morning Glory line of stoves beginning in 1852, while Philo Stewart of Troy patented his famous Stewart Stove that lifted the firebox off the floor to allow the flames to circulate evenly. The Stewart and many other improved stoves were manufactured in the mammoth Clinton Stove Works of the Fuller and Warren Company, which at one time shipped sixty thousand stoves, ranges and furnaces each year.

By 1875, Troy led the country with 260,000 stoves shipped annually, followed by Philadelphia (210,000) and Albany (198,000). However, the stove industry in the East began a gradual decline as manufacturing in general moved from New York and Pennsylvania to the West, where labor was cheaper and raw materials more plentiful. The last stove manufacturer, Burdett, Smith and Company of Troy, closed its doors in 1936, bringing the great era of stove making to an end.

ELIPHALET NOTT, SCHENECTADY

Anthracite Coal Stove

Although not an extensive stove manufacturer himself, Eliphalet Nott was a noted inventor who developed several early improvements that found their way into the designs of many thousands of stoves. He was born on June 25, 1773, in Ashford, Connecticut, where he received a basic education at home from his mother and later from his brother Samuel, who was a minister in the town of Franklin. He began teaching at a village school at the age of sixteen, and the following year he became the principal of Plainfield Academy. In 1796, he entered the Presbyterian ministry and was sent to Upstate New York to become a church pastor in Cherry Valley.

Five years later, Nott moved to Schenectady, where he became the fourth president of Union College at the age of thirty-one. Under his direction, the campus was greatly expanded and attained financial stability. He rewrote the curriculum and personally taught classes for several hours each day. An estimated four thousand students graduated from the college during his long career. In the meantime, he continued to give orations at the Presbyterian church in Albany and achieved some fame for a sermon he gave at the death of Alexander Hamilton.

Nott was an invento as well as a teacher. During his leisure time, he spent many hours in the laboratory conducting experiments on heating and steam engines. Over the years, he was awarded thirty patents, making him one of the most prolific inventors in the state until after the Civil War. They were among the so-called "X-patents" issued

Eliphalet Nott (1773–1866). *Courtesy of the Efner City History Center.*

before 1836 that were destroyed in the U.S. Patent Office fire. Fortunately, Nott replaced them at the request of Congress, so his patents are all on file in their entirety.

His heating inventions covered a variety of subjects, such as cooking and magazine stoves, steam furnaces, grates, stovepipes and water tubes. However, his greatest claim to fame was the invention of the first successful anthracite coal–burning stove, later known as the Nott Stove. Anthracite coal is harder and denser than regular coal and could not be kept ignited by the stoves then in use. Nott's first foray into stove design was a box stove in 1820 that was used to heat all of the Union College student rooms. Dealers

Eliphalet Nott's "Anthracite Coal Stove, Preventing the Escape of Heat from the Top of an Ignited Pile of Fuel."

in anthracite coal put out a call to inventors for a stove that could burn their product, and Nott answered in 1832 with a rectangular, illuminated magazine stove lined with fire-brick. Nott's patent was actually the third anthracite coal–burning stove patent, but his stove was the first one that actually worked as claimed.

In 1827, Nott and his son Henry established a foundry known as the Union Furnace on the corner of Washington and Central Avenues in Albany. Operating under the name Howard Nott and Company, it was soon manufacturing one thousand tons of stoves per year, almost half of the entire output of Albany. They were shipped around the country and overseas and were even praised in a short story by James Fenimore Cooper and in a poem by Oliver Wendell Holmes. Proceeds from the business were used to establish the Nott Trust Fund at Union College. Later, the company formed the Novelty Works in New York City for manufacturing Nott's steam boiler for powering boats and employed more than one thousand men by the 1850s.

Nott experienced much sorrow in his life. His mother passed away when he was only fifteen, and later he was forced to endure the deaths of his first two wives and only daughter. In 1852, an investigation was opened by Senator James Beekman when it was discovered that for years Nott had co-mingled the finances of Union College with his own. The investigation was later dropped and Nott was cleared of all charges, but the college's reputation suffered. In 1859, Nott suffered a paralytic stroke that all but ended his physical activities, although it was said that his inventive mind remained active. He remained the official college president until his death on January 29, 1866. Nott Road in Rexford, where his farm was located, is named after him, as is the beautiful Nott Memorial building located at the center of the Union College campus.

The Rathbone Family, Albany

Acorn Stove

There were a few stove makers operating in the Capital District prior to 1830, but the Rathbone family is generally given credit for establishing large-scale stove manufacturing in the region. In that year, Joel Rathbone started a small stove business on Quay Street, where he purchased castings made in Pennsylvania and assembled them to order. These castings were made from rough sand and were said to be very coarse and crude.

In 1835, Rathbone built the first foundry in the country that exclusively manufactured stoves. His castings were superior to those found elsewhere partly because of the high grade of sand found in the Hudson and Mohawk Valleys. By that time, his nephew, John Rathbone, had joined the firm and helped to enlarge its market around the country. Jared Rathbone became a partner for a time in the 1840s along with S.H. Ransom. After Joel retired, the firm went through a variety of partnership and name changes, but there was always at least one member of the Rathbone family involved. Clarence Rathbone purchased the stove works of S.H. Ransom and Company, a firm that was a descendant of the stove foundry first started by Joel Rathbone years earlier, and eventually combined it with the original Rathbone works. Lewis Rathbone joined the firm in 1854.

The Rathbone stoves proved to be widely successful. Reports of settlers heading west carrying their prized Rathbone stoves in their prairie wagons were plentiful. Wagonloads were sent across the Rocky Mountains to Utah for the followers of Brigham Young, while shiploads of stoves were sent around the African Cape of Good Hope to California during the gold rush. Branch houses were set up in Savannah, Buffalo and Chicago to serve markets in the southern and western parts of the country.

As head of the company, John Rathbone established several more foundries and spearheaded the development of new stoves and ranges. The firm's signature cooking stove was the Acorn series, featuring a new type of ventilation system that warmed the air before entering the oven, allowing it to easily pass into the flues and carry away smells and gases given off by the cooking. Hundreds of thousands of these stoves were shipped around the world over a number of decades. Another popular model was the Young American elevated stove series, patented in 1854, which featured two separate ovens with a flue that could direct heat to either oven or both. The Improved Chandelier Parlor Stove was able to burn coal or wood and won several awards for its superior design. Even after being on the market for four years, the company reported that it could not keep up with the demand for the Chandelier.

Several family members were involved with designing new stoves and patenting various improvements. John filed only the 142nd design patent in the country with his cooking stove. Lewis patented an improved circular coal stove consisting of only one fire chamber and vents in the sides of a suspended fire-pot to produce a hotter fire. Clarence patented a ventilating attachment that contained a screen for breaking up the flow of air. The separated air currents could be heated faster, making the stove more efficient. He also developed a method for installing two or more dampers that were synchronized with each other for ease of use.

The firm was incorporated in 1883 with a capital of $800,000 under the name Rathbone, Sard and Company and occupied an extensive land area with five cupola furnaces. Almost 1,500 laborers and molders were employed in the annual production of seventy-five thousand stoves valued at $1.5 million. The various foundries and partnerships of the Rathbone family were among the most successful in the country. They finally closed down the Albany location in 1925 after nearly a century of continuous operation.

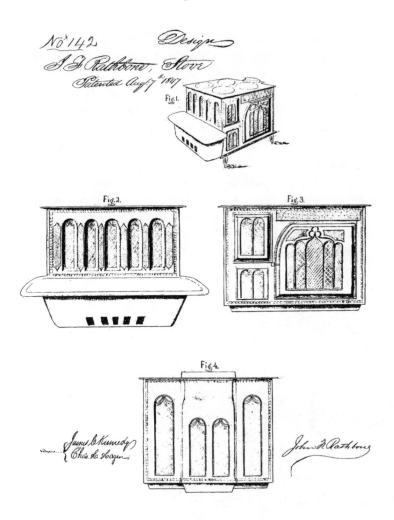

John Rathbone's "Design for a Stove."

DENNIS LITTLEFIELD, ALBANY

Morning Glory and West Shore Range Stoves

Dennis G. Littlefield was likely the most prolific inventor among the stove manufacturers of the Capital District. He had accumulated more than 150 patents at the time of his death, which put him among the top ten patent holders in the region. Among these were one of the first successful baseburner stoves, a popular anthracite coal–burning stove and dozens of both minor and significant improvements in the manufacture and design of stoves.

Littlefield began his career in the stove business with the baseburner stove noted above, patented in 1852. For a few years, he licensed the new heating stove to various manufacturers, particularly the firm of Jagger, Treadwell and Norton at the Eagle Stove Works. This partnership was a limited success, as the large chunks of coal used at that time weren't suited to his baseburner. He entered another partnership with future Albany mayor Erastus Corning to produce his patent Railway Coal Burner. Corning manufactured the heaters in his foundry and installed them on passenger cars of the New York Central Railroad. The heater's fifty-pound hopper held enough fuel to last the entire run between Albany and Buffalo and operated at one-tenth the

Advertisement for Dennis Littlefield's patent Morning Glory base burning coal stove. *Courtesy of the Library of Congress.*

cost of wood-fired stoves. Passengers were said to crowd into the cars that had the Littlefield heater, leaving other coaches nearly empty.

Building on his car heater success, in 1865 Littlefield established the Littlefield Stove Manufacturing Company and hired the Wasson Foundry on Montgomery Street to carry out the manufacturing arm of the business. When the New York Central Railroad extended its tracks in 1870, the Wasson Foundry had to be torn down. Littlefield used the opportunity to construct a large foundry of his own on the corner of North Pearl and Pleasant Streets that covered an area of three square acres.

Over the next few years, he expanded the Morning Glory line of stoves with dozens of patents to include cooking and parlor stoves, ranges and furnaces. The parlor stove in particular created a worldwide demand, and the foundry was unable to keep up with demand for it. One of its features was

Dennis Littlefield's "Improvement in Base Burning Stove."

the elimination of the back draft that would send smoke into the living area during windy weather. The channels of the stove were constructed so that they all flowed in one direction rather than meeting abruptly at one point before ascending the chimney. The stoves also had an improved, airtight damper design that retained much more heat when closed. His "swinging hearth" allowed an operator to move the entire hearth to the left for easy removal of the ash pan. It was also an effective anthracite-burning stove and was particularly popular wherever anthracite coal was used.

Littlefield's genius for inventing was well known in the area. The press normally placed him second only to Philo Stewart (described later) as the region's most influential inventor. It is especially noteworthy that he did not limit his attention to one aspect of stove technology. Several of his patents were for improvements on his original anthracite stove, but others were for cooking stoves, heating stoves, furnaces and railroad car heating systems. He also designed a variety of improved parts that could be used on any stove, such as grates, doors, flues and ash pans.

Sales of Littlefield's stoves increased steadily over the years, especially with the introduction of his Morning Glory stoves. Revenues jumped from $40,000 per year when the business opened to over $400,000 per year at its peak. He began producing the West Shore Range in 1884, which became so popular that it was soon the sole product of the business. The stove featured a double-grate, triple-oven door, boiling reservoir, double-sheet flue, oven shelf and thermometer, all of which were covered by separate patents. After Littlefield's death in 1899, the firm was carried on by his son, Major H.C. Littlefield. It was one of the longest-lived stove businesses in the region, finally closing in 1919 after more than fifty years of operation.

PHILO STEWART, TROY

The Stewart Stove

The life of Philo Penfield Stewart seems out of place with that of a traditional inventor, yet he was one of the most famous innovators of stoves in the history of Troy. He was born in 1798 in Sherman, Connecticut, but grew up in Pittsford, Vermont, apprenticing at the harness shop of his uncle. As an impressionable young man, he adopted many of the reform movements of the time, such as the antislavery and temperance movements. At the age of twenty-three, he enrolled with the American Missionary Board and set off

Philo Penfield
Stewart (1798–
1868). *Courtesy of
the Hudson Mohawk
Industrial Gateway,
Troy, New York.*

on horseback for the Mississippi River to engage in missionary work with the Choctaw Indians.

After a short time, Stewart made his way to Ohio and became reacquainted with one of his former schoolmates, the Reverend John Jay Shipherd. After a great deal of discussion and planning, the two men established the Oberlin Collegiate Institute in Ohio's Western Reserve. It was considered a radical experiment in education because the college was open not only to both sexes but to all races as well. Rather than charging for tuition, Stewart allowed the student body to work for its education.

In 1837, Stewart and his wife headed back east when he became disappointed with Oberlin's "lack of proper zeal and dedication." After developing an idea for a new stove design, he decided to relocate to Troy, which was gaining a reputation as a stove-making center. Upon arriving, he entered into an agreement with Fuller, Warren and Company, one of the city's largest stove foundries. Stewart provided the patented designs and

P. P. STEWART.

3 Sheets—Sheet 1.

Cooking Stove.

No. 1,684.

Reissued May 31, 1864.

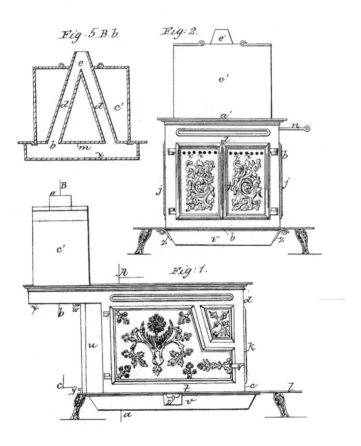

Witnesses.

Chas. D. Kellum
Marcus P. Norton

Inventor

Philo P. Stewart

Philo Stewart's "Improvement in Cooking Stove."

improvements, while Joseph Fuller and John Warren provided the means to manufacture the stoves in their Clinton Foundry.

It turned out to be a lucrative arrangement. Over the course of thirty years, approximately ninety thousand of his stoves were produced and sold around the country. Eliphalet Nott of Union College, inventor of the anthracite coal stove, was quoted as saying, "All that is of value in other stoves is taken from Stewart." The introduction of a new Stewart stove was apparently the cause of much fanfare. The *New York Times* reported one such occurrence in 1872 with the debut of his new Dumping Grate Stove: "The stove store was visited by hundreds of citizens, including many from adjoining towns, to witness the prodigies performed by one of Stewart's latest cooking stoves. The stove itself is a marvel of economy and convenience, and it performed all and more than the agents claimed for it."

Reviews of cooking stoves indicated that his were more effective than others on the market. One of Stewart's important improvements consisted of a design that used the front plate of the firebox to warm the air as it was drawn into a chamber behind the front doors. The warmed air was used for improved ventilation and to shorten the cooking time. His "Summer and Winter Cooking Stoves" were designed to burn both coal and wood so that they could be used in any season. He also patented a series of coal stoves that were designed to quickly ventilate the smoke from bituminous or other gaseous coal. He was revered in the press as "having revolutionized the stove business in America."

Based primarily on Stewart's patents, Fuller, Warren and Company became one of the largest stove manufacturers in the region. It grew throughout the late 1800s to occupy a large, six-acre plot bounded by Madison, River and Monroe Streets and employ over 1,200 men. Salesrooms were established in New York City, Boston, Cleveland and Chicago, while a second foundry was built in Milwaukee, Wisconsin, to accommodate the western demand for the Stewart stoves.

Most individuals who make their living from inventions are preoccupied with developing new ones, but Stewart did not fit this mold. Although he had numerous patents for a variety of cooking stoves and parts, he invested most of his time and money in helping others. He donated funds to operate a school for illiterate servant girls, financially supported Oberlin College and cared for the poor and sick in and around Troy. His death on December 13, 1868, was widely mourned throughout the city.

LIGHTING THE WORLD

The name General Electric may be well known in the world today, but its overwhelming influence on the lives of nearly every person in the country during the 1900s can only be appreciated by students of history or those who lived during the era of electrical development. Until GE began downsizing its operations in the 1970s, the city of Schenectady was a household name and known as the "City that Lights and Hauls the World."

General Electric was formed in 1892 when two of the largest electric companies—the Edison Electric Company of Thomas Edison and the Thomson-Houston Electric Company of Elihu Thomson—joined together. Although GE had plants in Massachusetts and New Jersey, Edison decided that Schenectady had competitive advantages in transportation, workforce and geography, so the city would be the location of the principal operations and manufacturing centers.

Within just ten years of its incorporation, General Electric was the largest manufacturer of electrical machinery in the world. Over sixteen thousand people were employed in a campus that contained 150 factory buildings. The "city within a city" had its own firehouse, restaurants, police force, telephone system and even a private hospital. By mid-century, the workforce had increased to thirty thousand.

The GE campus was designed to house every aspect of the production of extremely complex machinery. The drafting department employed four hundred people and contained 250,000 drawings. The brass foundry was equipped with sixteen compressed air molding machines to produce 2,100 tons of castings per year. The iron foundry was housed in a 150,000-square-

Charles Steinmetz (center) and other scientists at General Electric. Also pictured is Albert Einstein, who visited the facility in 1921, the same year that he won the Nobel Prize in physics. *Courtesy of the Library of Congress.*

foot building with giant cranes for maneuvering the heavy product from the storage yard to the shop. Some of the largest buildings were the machine shops. Building No. 16 alone covered an area of three and a half square acres. In the testing department, six hundred students from dozens of universities tested various machinery to complete their education. Other buildings were devoted to turbines, transformers, electric locomotives, searchlights, wiring and rheostats.

The company was considered to be at the forefront of technology during the early 1900s. The *Electrical Handbook* wrote, "Never before in the history of manufacturing has such progress been recorded. Invention followed invention, discovery followed discovery, until it seemed as though the public was introduced to new electrical marvels every day." Over one thousand gifted inventors devoted all of their time toward the continual refinement of current technologies and the development of new ones. A large staff of patent lawyers was kept busy processing the thousands of patents assigned to the company. In 1978, GE celebrated the awarding of its 50,000[th] patent.

Just a few of its numerous breakthroughs in science included the carbon filament lamp, the first voice radio broadcast, the ductile tungsten filament for incandescent lamps, the first electric range, the first electric-powered warship and the first commercially successful refrigerator. Understandably, only a small sampling of the many talented scientists and inventors of GE can be represented in a book of this kind. Many famous inventors could not be included, especially those who were active in the years after the Great Depression. However, those that follow represent the most noteworthy of the scientists who were instrumental in shaping the company in the early years and had the greatest influence on GE's expansion into one of history's largest corporations.

The first inventor in this chapter, Joseph Henry of Albany, was not an employee of General Electric and, in fact, passed away before GE was formed. However, Henry was an important scientist, paving the way for the invention of the telegraph as well as setting a precedent for innovation in the Capital District.

JOSEPH HENRY, ALBANY

Electromagnet

One of the Capital District's greatest inventors was unusual in that he never patented any of his inventions. Although he often stated that he never regretted this decision, it deprived him of a vast fortune and an even higher place among the world's great scientists. Joseph Henry was born on December 17, 1797, in Albany and spent several years in the Saratoga County village of Galway. Later, he studied at the Albany Academy, taught at a district school in Selkirk for two years and was a tutor at the Van Rensselaer Manor House.

Henry's career as an inventor began in 1826 when he became professor of natural sciences at the Albany Academy. Between classes, he began to experiment with the relationship between electricity and magnets. He created what he termed an "intensity magnet," the first one ever made. Until that time, scientists around the world declared that electrical power and electrical signals, such as what would be used in a telegraph, were impossible to create. Henry's invention was one of the most significant of the century, simply because it allowed electricity to be conveyed over long distances.

The idea for an electromagnet occurred to him after studying the experiments of the famous French scientist Andre-Marie Ampere. Ampere

Joseph Henry (1797–1878).
*Courtesy of the Library of
Congress.*

wrapped a wire around a soft iron bar to generate a magnetic force. The basis
of Henry's improvement was in wrapping a much longer wire, measuring
sixty feet, around the iron bar. The result was an electromagnet far more
powerful than had ever been made. He then applied a small galvanic battery
for still greater power. Further refinements were made with copper wire, zinc
plating, different types of batteries and different sizes of wires. The result
was an intensity magnet that carried electricity over long distances with very
little loss of power. In addition, the small device had the capability of lifting
a one-thousand-pound weight.

Henry followed up these experiments with a second milestone toward
the creation of the telegraph. He stumbled upon a way of transmitting
signals over long distances by striking a lever of metal against a wire. He
hung up a mile of wire around one of the upper rooms at the Albany
Academy and set up a magnetized steel bar between the two arms of a

horseshoe magnet. When the current traveled through the wire, the bar struck one end of the magnet, making a bell sound. This was widely considered to be the first electromagnetic telegraph that worked through a wire of any significant length.

Henry's disregard for either applying his discoveries toward a practical application or patenting his ideas weighed on his legacy. He later admitted that he was not an inventor in the sense that he could make a discovery and then adapt it to real world situations. He was content to advance science beyond the limits of current thought and let others figure out how to make his advancements useful in everyday life.

One of those people would turn out to be Samuel Morse. Professor Leonard Gale, who was helping Morse at the time, mentioned Henry's discoveries in electromagnetism. The pair quickly concluded that this was the breakthrough they needed to overcome the limitations of transmitting electric signals. Morse consulted Henry in person on several occasions for advice and encouragement. When Morse asked the government for $30,000 to run a telegraph line between Washington, D.C., and Baltimore, Henry's opinion was sought as to the feasibility of such an endeavor. Some sources claim that the government would not have funded the experiment if Henry had given a negative opinion.

Although Morse would later play down Henry's role in the invention of the telegraph, Henry made several advancements without which the telegraph could not have been practical. He was the first to fully develop electromagnetism using soft iron; the first to employ a galvanic battery to project electric current through wire; the first to use a long wire to receive the current; the first to magnetize a piece of iron at a distance; and the first to project a sound at great distance using an electromagnet.

Henry did not seek fame or fortune from his discoveries. After submitting his improvements in sending signals through wire, he was quoted as saying, "The only reward I ever expected was the consciousness of advancing science, the pleasure of discovering new truths, and the scientific reputation to which these labors entitle me. I never myself attempted to reduce these principles to practice or to apply any of my discoveries to processes in the arts." Had Henry patented all of his discoveries, Morse and many others would have been obliged to pay him royalties for every telegraphic instrument manufactured. In his writings, it does not appear that Henry ever regretted his decision.

Henry's electromagnet also directly inspired the invention of the first electric motor. One of his electromagnets was installed at the Penfield Iron Works at Crown Point, New York, for separating magnetic ore. A Vermont inventor named Thomas Davenport heard of the device and traveled to the facility to purchase some iron for his blacksmith shop. When he saw Henry's machine in action, he became so fascinated that he instead purchased the electromagnet. After hundreds of experiments, Davenport was able to modify the device to produce rotary motion as a source of power and, in so doing, invented the first primitive electric motor.

In 1832, soon after his most important discoveries had been perfected, Henry was offered a job at Princeton University, followed by another offer to become the first head of the new Smithsonian Institute in Washington. He left Albany, never to return. In the years that followed, he helped to establish the American Association for the Advancement of Science, serving as its president. In 1862, he sat for Christian Schussele's famous portrait of the nation's nineteen greatest living inventors, called *Men of Progress* (local inventors Eliphalet Nott and Henry Burden are also in the painting). Some call Henry the father of daily weather forecasts for his work in establishing six hundred observation stations around the country. He passed away in Washington on May 13, 1878, and is recognized as one of history's greatest scientists and inventors. The former Albany Academy building where Henry made his most famous discoveries, located opposite city hall, has since been renamed the Joseph Henry Memorial Building.

CHARLES STEINMETZ, SCHENECTADY

Alternating Current

Perhaps General Electric's most unique and gifted scientist was German native Charles Proteus Steinmetz. His groundbreaking research and long list of patented inventions—many of which are still used in electrical technology today—greatly expanded the role of electrical power. Steinmetz was born on April 9, 1865, in Breslau, Germany. He was afflicted from birth with dwarfism and kyphosis (a curvature of the spine) but amazed his teachers from an early age with his understanding of mathematics and physics. However, just as he was about to earn his doctorate at the University of Breslau, the German police began investigating his participation in socialist activities. Because socialism was banned at that time, Steinmetz felt compelled to leave the country and immigrate to the United States.

Upon his arrival in this country, he began working with Rudolf Eickemeyer of New York City developing transformers, which are used to transmit

Charles Steinmetz
(1865–1923). *Courtesy of
the Library of Congress.*

electricity. General Electric manager Edwin Rice heard of his abilities and tried to persuade him to relocate to Schenectady. At first Steinmetz declined, so Rice asked GE management to purchase the business and patents of Eickemeyer's company. This done, Steinmetz moved to Schenectady in 1894, where he was promoted to direct the Calculating Department. One of his roles was to solve mathematical problems brought to him by other scientists who were unable to solve them.

His first of many patents was for a system of alternating current distribution that used motors capable of running without multiphase generators. This would prove to be one of his most important inventions, leading to his induction into the National Inventors Hall of Fame. His lecture on the subject at the International Electrical Congress in Chicago was the first time anyone had explained alternating current phenomena in public.

Other research focused on the production and control of man-made lightning. One source claims that his interest in the subject stemmed from a

(No Model.)　　　　　　　　　　　　　　　　2 Sheets—Sheet 1.

C. P. STEINMETZ.
SYSTEM OF DISTRIBUTION BY ALTERNATING CURRENTS.

No. 533,244.　　　　　　　　　　Patented Jan. 29, 1895.

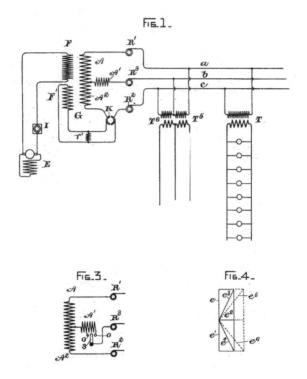

WITNESSES.
a. F. Macdonald
B. B. Hill.

INVENTOR—
Charles P. Steinmetz
By Geo. R. Blodgett
atty.

Charles Steinmetz's "System of Distribution by Alternating Currents."

lightning strike at his camp near the Mohawk River. A building the size of a football field served as his laboratory for creating the world's first artificial lightning using 120,000-volt generators. His work in this field made him known as the "forger of thunderbolts."

Another field of study was his work in a subject called electrical motor "hysteresis," or systems that have memory. For example, the motor that operates a furnace is either on or off, with nothing in between. The introduction of a thermostat provides the memory required to maintain a constant temperature. Steinmetz applied the concept of hysteresis to a multitude of applications useful to industry. He also designed the first magnetite arc lamp. By using electrodes made of carbon instead of iron oxide and titanium, the power and life of the arc lamp were significantly increased.

His part-time position as professor at Union College, research into lightning and role as problem solver for other scientists would be more than enough for most people, but Steinmetz also managed to conduct his own groundbreaking research into electrical motors, dynamos and alternating current distribution, resulting in the accumulation of over two hundred patents. Steinmetz even found time to write thirteen books and sixty articles on a range of subjects. One of the most influential books on electricity in history was his *Theory of Calculation of Alternating Current Phenomena*, written in 1897 with the assistance of Ernst Berg. When he tried to become a Schenectady alderman on the Socialist ticket, the bemused but respectful *New York Times* called him "one of the world's greatest scientists." He passed away on October 26, 1923, and is buried in Schenectady's Vale Cemetery. GE called his passing "the end of the Steinmetz Era."

ERNST ALEXANDERSON, SCHENECTADY

High-Frequency Alternator

Among General Electric's most prolific inventors was Ernst Frederick Alexanderson, owner of an astounding 344 patents. He was born in Sweden on January 25, 1878, and was educated at the Royal Institute of Technology in Stockholm. While visiting Germany, he read Charles Steinmetz's book *Theory of Calculation of Alternating Current Phenomena*. Alexanderson was so inspired that he decided to immigrate to America and secure a position with Steinmetz in the Consulting Engineering Department.

In 1905, Alexanderson submitted his first six patents. Each one that he submitted was followed by a second, related patent that slightly modified the previous one. Once the related patent was approved, it would lead to others in a long chain that spanned his entire career and into retirement. There could be several of these "patent families" in development at any given time.

While most other inventors concentrate on one subject, Alexanderson displayed a remarkable ability to research and develop inventions in many different fields. His most important work involved improvements to alternators and motors, but he also submitted patents for electric ship propulsion, electric railway systems, telephone relays, gun control systems and improvements in analog computers, radio and television.

Radio pioneer Reginald Fessenden attempted to build an alternating generator that could attain a frequency of 100,000 Hertz at a time when the

Ernst Alexanderson (1878–1975). *Sebring Collection, courtesy of the Efner City History Center.*

standard generator produced fewer than 100 Hertz. When his experiments failed, he turned to GE and Alexanderson for help. Agreeing to take on the challenge, Alexanderson devoted all of his energy to the project. He submitted a patent for a high-frequency alternator in 1916 that could produce currents of up to 100,000 cycles, as Fessenden requested.

Over the following decade, Alexanderson developed such an effective alternator, capable of transmitting messages across the Atlantic for the first time, that it was installed in the famous Marconi radio station in New Brunswick and used by President Wilson during World War I. Guglielmo Marconi, the founder of the England-based Marconi Company, visited GE and made an offer to purchase the exclusive right to sell the alternator. President Wilson himself appealed to GE to decline the offer, fearing that Great Britain would come to dominate the market. As a result, the Radio

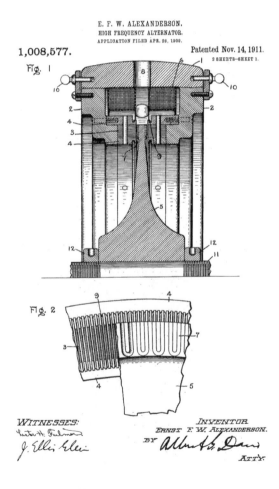

Ernst Alexanderson's "High Frequency Alternator."

Corporation of America (RCA) was established in the United States to market the alternators. For a few years, Alexanderson worked at both GE and RCA as its chief engineer before returning to GE full time. The tuning device later became an integral part of modern radio systems and led to his admission into the Inventors Hall of Fame.

Alexanderson's huge patent portfolio contained many important improvements in radio technology. Among the most famous of these were the magnetic amplifier, the multiple-tuned antenna, the antistatic receiving antenna and the directional transmitting antenna. In order to build the first electronic amplifier, he borrowed the modified vacuum tubes invented by colleague Irving Langmuir and applied them to radio telephony. The tubes became the basis for all future radio broadcasting.

While his high-frequency alternator is perhaps Alexanderson's most significant patent, his distinguished career held many other achievements. He was the first to transmit a facsimile message across the Atlantic Ocean. In 1927, he staged the first home reception of television from his residence in Schenectady, and the following year he gave the first public demonstration of television. Of his 344 patents, 11 were private, 34 were developed with others and the rest were assigned to GE. His last patent was submitted at the age of ninety-five. He passed away two years later and is buried in Schenectady's Vale Cemetery.

WILLIAM COOLIDGE, SCHENECTADY

Ductile Tungsten

The history of ductile tungsten may not be the subject of popular bedtime stories, but its discovery by William Coolidge had a significant impact on a wide array of applications over the last century, from X-rays to ignition systems to lighting. His innovations have directly affected the lives of millions of people since his first patent was awarded.

Coolidge was born in Hudson, Massachusetts, on October 23, 1873. After graduating from the Massachusetts Institute of Technology with a bachelor of science degree, he traveled to Leipzig, Germany, to earn his doctorate. Upon returning to the United States, he worked as a researcher before joining General Electric's Research Laboratory in 1905, becoming assistant director of the department three years later.

William Coolidge (1873–1975), *far right*, along with Irving Langmuir and Willis Whitney, director of the GE Research Lab. *Courtesy of the Library of Congress.*

At the time of his arrival, GE was attempting to create a better filament than the inefficient carbon loops that were in use. Several scientists were working with tungsten at the same time, both in the United States and in Europe. However, no one had been able to bend the metal once it was formed into a wire, so it was universally known as being a non-ductile metal. Coolidge discovered that very thin strands of tungsten could be constructed by building up a wire with grains of the metal cemented together with paraffin. After passing an electrical current through the strand, the paraffin was melted away and the grains of metal would be fused together. In his 1912 patent, Coolidge wrote, "I have been able to produce from this refractory, brittle, non-ductile material and generally unworkable metal a wire which is tough, fibrous, and elastic and of high tensile strength."

The new tungsten wire was immediately applied to light bulbs and incandescent lamps. Soon Coolidge's tungsten wires were found in almost every light bulb, and they are still in wide use today. GE sold Coolidge's lamp under the trade name "Mazda" and advertised it extensively throughout the country. The long-lasting and efficient light bulb helped the company win back its dominance in the field of electricity after Thomas Edison's early patents had begun to expire.

Coolidge's next project was X-ray technology. This time he used his tungsten as a target material. The result of his experiments was a new vacuum tube that made X-rays safe enough for use in medical situations. For example, Coolidge devised a portable X-ray machine that was utilized in field hospitals during World War I. Another of his devices aided the United States Navy during the war by detecting enemy submarines. He made further improvements to the submarine detector that led to the "K" tube, which had a range of ten miles and was instrumental in halting the destruction of Allied shipping by German submarines. The first submarine hunt in history was conducted by a British warship in 1918 using Coolidge's detector. Another version of the invention was a dental X-ray that consisted of a shielded tube with a fifty-six-thousand-volt transformer, all contained within a sealed case for safety.

Coolidge was well known for his modesty, kindness and integrity throughout his long career. After twenty years as assistant director, he was successively promoted to associate director, director and finally vice-president and director of research in 1940. He retired from GE four years later but remained as a consultant. At the age of one hundred, he was elected to the National Inventors Hall of Fame as the holder of eighty-three patents. He passed away in Schenectady the following year on February 4, 1975.

W. D. COOLIDGE.

TUNGSTEN AND METHOD OF MAKING THE SAME FOR USE AS FILAMENTS OF INCANDESCENT
ELECTRIC LAMPS AND FOR OTHER PURPOSES.

APPLICATION FILED JUNE 19, 1912.

1,082,933.

Patented Dec. 30, 1913.

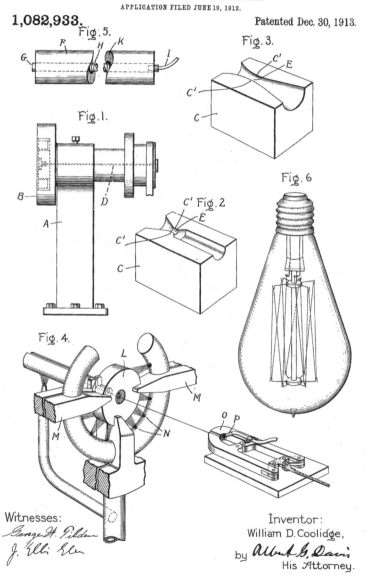

Witnesses:
George H. Tilden
J. Ellis Glen

Inventor:
William D. Coolidge,
by Albert G. Davis
His Attorney.

William Coolidge's "Tungsten and Method of Making the Same for Use of Filaments."

WILLIAM EMMET, SCHENECTADY

Electric Turbines for Warships

As a consulting engineer for General Electric, William LeRoy Emmet spent years studying the subject of powering ships with electricity. He was finally able to prove that it was both economical and practical to do so, resulting in its adoption by the United States Navy on large warships.

Emmet was born on July 10, 1859, in Pelham, New York, and attended schools in both the United States and Canada before entering the U.S. Naval Academy in 1881. After resigning from the navy, he earned seven dollars per week as a laborer for the United States Illuminating Company. He next worked at the Sprague Electric Railway and Motor Company, just as Frank Sprague was developing the world's first reliable electric trolley. A few years later, he accepted a position with the Edison General Electric Company. When Thomas Edison merged his company with a former rival to form General Electric, Emmet moved to Schenectady and began his career of experimentation and invention.

His first project was improving upon the Curtis steam turbine engine. Charles Curtis developed the turbine in 1896 and assigned the patent to General Electric. Emmet worked with Curtis for five years to improve upon the design and adapt it to be constructed as a large power turbine. In his biography, Emmet claimed, "We developed an enormous industry and put nearly every other engine builder in the country out of business so far as the driving of electrical apparatus was concerned."

A natural progression into electrical ship propulsion followed, as the electric turbines he was developing were well suited for powering large ships. Part of his research involved vaporizing mercury rather than water within the turbine engine. The vaporized mercury powered one turbine and, while cooling, would convert water into vapor, which powered a second turbine, all in one process.

Once Emmet's improvements were completed, the United States Navy used his ideas to build new warships. The first electrically propelled navy vessel, a twenty-thousand-ton collier named the *Jupiter*, was completed in 1912. Installation of its 7,000-horsepower turbine generator was personally supervised by Emmet. Three years later, the navy completed its first all electric ship. The thirty-two-thousand-ton battleship, named *New Mexico*, had two 15,000-horsepower turbines that powered all of the ship's services. Later, GE installed Emmet's drive systems on the high-speed battle cruisers known

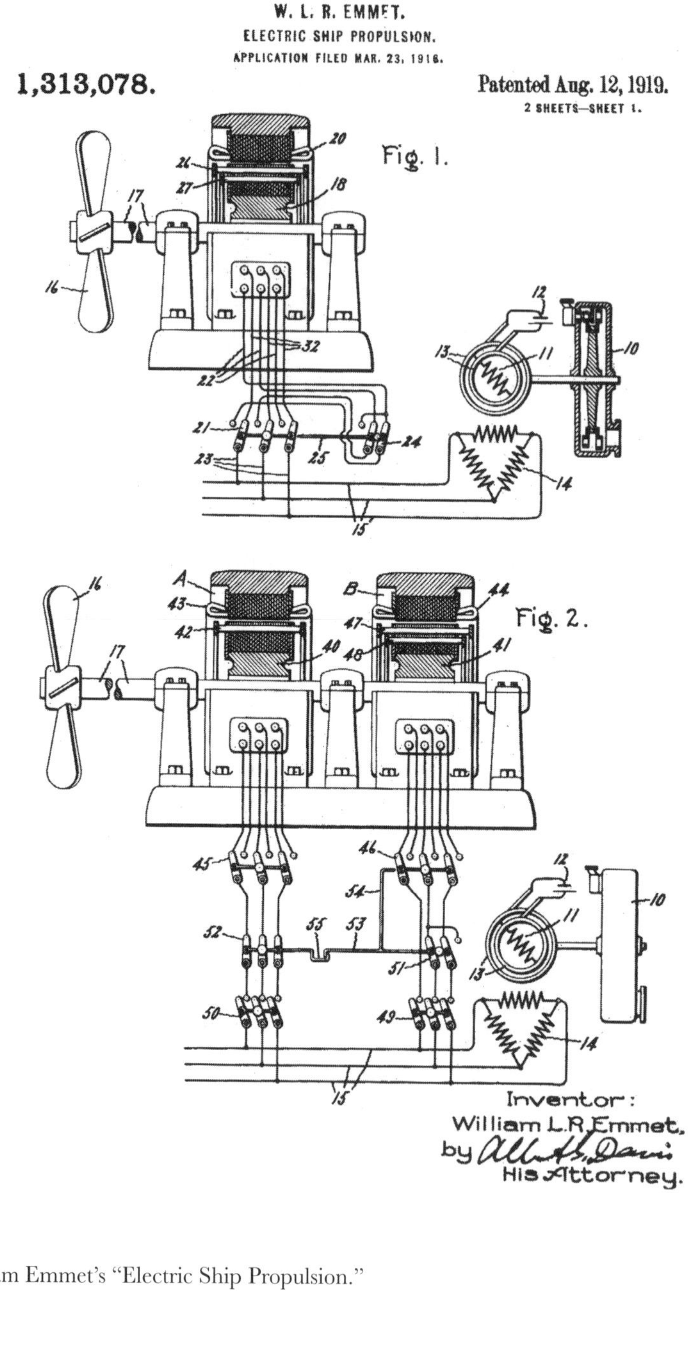

W. L. R. EMMET.
ELECTRIC SHIP PROPULSION.
APPLICATION FILED MAR. 23, 1916.

1,313,078.

Patented Aug. 12, 1919.
2 SHEETS—SHEET 1.

Fig. 1.

Fig. 2.

Inventor:
William L. R. Emmet.
by *Albert G. Davis*
His Attorney.

William Emmet's "Electric Ship Propulsion."

as the *Saratoga* and *Lexington*, which could generate 180,000 horsepower and cruise at thirty-five knots.

Other inventions developed during his career at General Electric included varnished cambric insulation, an oil switch, a flywheel for stabilizing gyroscopes on warships, a solar heater, forced air circulation and several types of transformers and transformer parts. In contrast to his boss, Thomas Edison, who pushed hard for direct current to become the accepted form of electric transmission, Emmet helped to develop alternating current, which was supported by Edison's rival George Westinghouse.

Although he was given several lucrative offers to leave Schenectady and GE, Emmet was never tempted and even turned down offers of promotion within GE. He was content to conduct experiments in his lab and let others shoulder the responsibility of management and vision. In his spare time, he wrote such books as *The Formation of the Earth and the Moon* and *Alternating Current Wiring and Distribution*. He won many prestigious awards for his work, including the Edison Medal and gold medals at both the St. Louis and San Francisco expositions. He died on September 26, 1941, with a total of 122 patents.

IRVING LANGMUIR, SCHENECTADY

Incandescent Light Bulbs

There are only a few Nobel Prize winners who worked or lived in the Capital District, but two of them worked at General Electric: Ivan Giaever and Irving Langmuir. The latter was one of the most famous industrial scientists of the twentieth century and developed a long list of inventions that directly affect millions of people to this day. Some have compared his contributions to those of Thomas Edison.

Langmuir was born in New York City on July 31, 1881. His father was a traveling salesman, and as such, the family frequently moved around the country and throughout Europe. Despite the lack of a consistent schooling schedule, Langmuir was able to graduate from Columbia University with a degree in metallurgical engineering at the age of twenty-two. He developed a love of chemistry from his older brother Arthur and decided to pursue a PhD in Germany under Nobel Laureate Walther Nernst.

Upon returning to the United States, Langmuir joined the Stevens Institute of Technology in New Jersey for research and teaching. He soon became

Irving Langmuir (1881–1957) in his laboratory. *Courtesy of the Library of Congress.*

frustrated because he was unable to carry out the research he wanted. He spent his summer vacation in 1909 doing some research at General Electric. Willis Whitney, the director of the research lab, recognized his potential and persuaded him to work for the company permanently.

Langmuir's first set of experiments was perhaps the most important of his career. Nearly every scientist, including Thomas Edison, was convinced that the best way to manufacture a long-lasting light bulb was to create a perfect vacuum within the bulb. Langmuir discovered that by filling the light bulb with an inert gas, such as argon, it would last much longer. This discovery has saved consumers untold millions of dollars in replacing light bulbs and is considered to be the advent of the modern electric light bulb. During these experiments, he pioneered the concept of conducting fundamental research rather than using the trial-and-error methods preferred by Edison and other GE scientists, evoking an overall change in culture of the research laboratory.

His work in light bulbs led to experiments with vacuum pumps, atomic hydrogen, smoke generators, cloud seeding and high-temperature heat transfer. He introduced the concept of electron temperature and invented the diagnostic method for measuring it using an electrostatic probe. Now called the Langmuir Probe, it is commonly used in plasma physics. Langmuir was the first person to use the word "plasma" in a physics application, a word he used because the ionized gases he was working with reminded him of blood plasma.

In 1923, he developed the process of atomic hydrogen welding that permitted the joining of many metals that had been difficult to weld. However, the path to winning the 1932 Nobel Prize began with a series of experiments in partnership with Katharine Blodgett to study thin films and how substances are absorbed on the surface. He discovered the existence of monolayers, or surface films of a single atom of thickness. For his groundbreaking work, Langmuir was not only the first person to win a Nobel Prize in surface chemistry but was also the first industrial scientist to be awarded.

Despite the fact that most of his experiments were not patentable, Langmuir was able to amass sixty-three patents during his time at GE, as well as write 229 publications. He was awarded twenty-one medals and awards and received honorary degrees from fifteen schools, including Oxford, Harvard and Princeton. In the same year he won the Nobel Prize, he was nominated Man of the Year by *TIME* magazine and graced the covers of many other magazines. He died of a heart attack on August 16, 1957. His house on Stratford Road in Schenectady was declared a National Historic Landmark in 1976.

FIRE AND WATER

Although the Mohawk and Hudson Rivers converged in the Waterford area, the flow of water was too slow to power machinery. Therefore, there was little opportunity to develop industry until a system of canals was constructed beginning in the 1820s. A wide variety of industry sprang up once the Champlain and King's Canals were finished through Waterford, much of which was unique to Upstate New York.

The manufacture of fire engines began in Albany and was relocated to Waterford on the new King's Canal. The factory was first operated by John Rogers, but a talented inventor named Lysander Button assumed control and expanded it to become one of the region's most famous companies. Hundreds of communities at one time or another owned a Button fire engine. As late as 1900, there were fewer than ten major fire engine manufacturers in the country, illustrating the complexity and specialty of this industry.

Another industry not found in the region outside of the Waterford-Troy area was the manufacture of water valves. Valves have been used for hundreds of years to control the flow of water through pipes, although the biggest impetus for improvement came only with the advent of the steam engine. It is not known why Troy became one of the country's few valve-manufacturing centers. It is likely that if not for the valve innovations and patents of George Eddy and Henry Ludlow, the industry would never have developed there.

Eddy invented a popular model about twenty-five years after opening the Mohawk and Hudson Foundry on the King's Canal. Eddy also patented an improved fire hydrant, which is essentially a large valve. Hydrants were sold in huge volumes during the mid-1800s as cities began installing them for the first time. Over eighty thousand were installed in New York City alone.

Ludlow invented a valve of his own and enjoyed great success beginning in the 1860s. By the time Ludlow sold his share of the company to a group of New York City investors, it was the largest valve company in the country. The effectiveness of Ludlow's invention kept the foundry competitive until 1969. Two other valve manufacturers, Ross Valve and the Rensselaer Valve Manufacturing Company, were established in Troy after Ludlow was already a nationwide success.

These industries were also unique in that all of the success and longevity of the individual businesses were due to the inventions of their owners. Competition from valve and fire engine manufacturers around the country would have quickly crushed those of the Capital District if the owners did not invent groundbreaking products that created high demand in the market. Valves were a particularly tough sell, as cities were prone to using just one vendor for all of their valves. It would have taken a unique and effective design for a municipal administrator to commit to an unknown vendor. Lysander Button's fire engines also faced rigorous testing from firemen who required reliable equipment that was easy to use and maneuver. The fact that the several valve manufacturers and one fire engine manufacturer survived for so long and were so successful in an area where few others existed is testament to the talent of the inventors who established them.

LYSANDER BUTTON, WATERFORD

Hand and Steam Fire Engines

One of the most famous and long-lived Waterford businesses was the Button Fire Engine Works, which derived all of its success from the dozens of patented fire engine improvements of its namesake, Lysander Button. Button was born on September 2, 1810, in North Haven, Connecticut, and came to Albany with his parents at the age of fifteen. He became familiar with fire engines at the machine shop of John Rogers of Waterford. Button remained at the shop after it was sold to William Platt and Judge Nicholas Doe and became a partner by 1834. Platt later sold his share to Button, who became sole owner upon the death of Judge Doe.

Button displayed a genius for mechanical innovation. He developed the first "piano engine," which featured an improved water delivery system;

the first "runaround" that returned water to the suction to relieve pressure on the hose; the first water pump; the first folding brakes; the first engine with a permanent suction hose; and a "crane neck" side-stroke engine. Unfortunately, none of these improvements was patented, which not only deprived future generations of the specifications but also allowed others to copy Button's designs with impunity.

Thereafter, Button went through the patent process to protect his ideas. The first ten or so were developed with his business partner, Robert Blake, who joined the firm in 1857. About this time, the first steam-powered fire engines were beginning to make their debut, and Button immediately recognized the potential of these to be much more effective than the old-fashioned hand pumpers. Within a few years of Blake's admittance to the firm, the engine was ready for its first public demonstration. Hundreds of people gathered to see the curiosity as it shot water high into the air. It was sold to the city of Battle Creek, Michigan, where it served the community well for many years.

The Button Fire Engine Works flourished throughout the latter 1800s, selling thousands of hand and steam fire engines throughout the United States, Canada, South America and Europe. Dozens of local towns and villages had at least one Button engine, including Albany, Troy, Saratoga Springs, Ballston Spa and Schenectady. Six different sizes were made, ranging from four thousand to six thousand pounds, featuring upright boilers, copper tubing, metal construction and all of Button's many improvements.

The construction of the vehicle body was also patented. The engine was kept separate from the frame and running gear so that rough roads would not damage the machinery. The steam cylinder and pump were secured in their relative positions by a casting that formed a head for each. These improvements greatly increased the efficiency of the vehicle and added strength and durability. Only five pounds of steam were needed to draw and throw water, and twenty pounds of steam would throw water to a height of 90 feet. At full steam, water could be thrown up to 265 feet. The arrangement of the steam pump upon the forward wheels and the boiler on the rear wheels, with the two sets of wheels connected by a light crane neck of iron, was also patented. Button even mixed his own metal to manufacture his fire engines, using Bessemer steel from Troy so that no part would corrode over time. The Button Steamer won the Centennial Award at the 1876 Philadelphia International Exhibition for its simplicity, strength and reliability.

After spending almost half a century manufacturing fire engines, Lysander decided to retire in 1882 and sell the entire works, including the rights to his

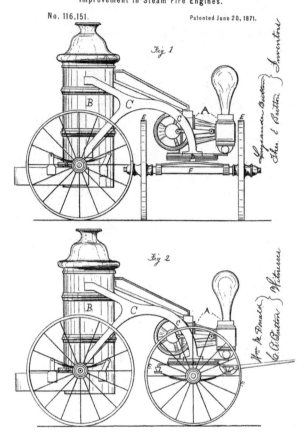

L. BUTTON & T. E. BUTTON.

Improvement in Steam Fire Engines.

No. 116,151.   Patented June 20, 1871.

Lysander Button's "Improvement in Steam Fire Engines."

many patents, to Holroyd and Company of Waterford. In 1900, all of the major fire engine companies were consolidated into the American LaFrance Fire Engine Company, which continues to operate today.

Button passed away on July 19, 1898, at the age of eighty-eight. As firefighting technology advanced during the twentieth century, fewer and fewer Button engines were left in existence. Fortunately, the Waterford Historical Museum and Cultural Center was able to obtain an 1857 Button and Blake hand pumper called the "Converse" so that history fans now and in the future may see an original Button fire engine in person.

GEORGE EDDY, WATERFORD

Mohawk Hydrant and Eddy Valve

The Eddy family of Waterford possibly had more inventors than any other family in the Capital District. Isaac Eddy, the patriarch, was born in Weathersfield, Vermont, and had thirteen children. While living in Vermont, he invented a process for pulverizing the ingredients of printers' ink. After relocating to Waterford in 1826, he established the Franklin Ink Works. His son Thomas Jefferson Eddy derived a formula for colored ink that he used to manufacture "lamp black" at the Franklin Works when the manufacture of ink was discontinued. Another son named Oliver Tarbell Eddy invented a typewriting machine in 1850.

Even more successful was Isaac's third son, George Washington Eddy. Born in 1811, George moved with the rest of his family to Waterford and worked with his father and brother at the Ink Works. At the age of twenty-three, he submitted one of Saratoga County's earliest patents—an improved boat hull. Unfortunately, this was one of the X-patents that was lost to fire in 1836 and never replaced. Some of his other inventions included two different railroad car wheels, an improvement in railroad cars that provided

The Eddy Valve Company foundry. *Courtesy of the Waterford Museum and Cultural Center.*

for additional wheels to be added for extra safety, a raised star design for stove plates, a hollow oven door, an improved bridle bit, a neck yoke, a fish plate connection for rail joints and a steam heating system for railroad cars.

The impetus for some of these inventions came from Eddy's production line at the Mohawk and Hudson Manufacturing Company, which he established in 1847. At first, the company produced car wheels and iron castings. As time went on and the manufacturing process was refined, other items were added to the product listing, such as wine and straw presses, lathe chucks, axes, hitching posts and cast-iron statuary. The foundry produced a stunning quantity of castings, including six thousand stoves in its first year of operation. By the age of forty-nine, George Eddy was one of the wealthiest people in Saratoga County, with a fortune that would be worth over $2 million today.

His wealth only increased with the release of his most successful inventions. In 1873, he patented his world-famous taper-seat, double-gate valve. The Eddy Valve consisted of two gates and a piece called the ball. The gates were hung with two trunnions on the ball that allowed the gates to revolve freely. This caused them to seat in a different position every time to prevent them from becoming worn out in one spot. At the base of each trunnion there was a convex surface that fit into the concave surface on the back of the gates, which permitted the gates to adjust themselves to their tapered seat. This assembly created a tight and long-lasting fit that no water could penetrate. Eddy also perfected a parallel-seat, double-gate valve, a straightway valve and a check-valve that kept water from flowing backward in case of a pipe break.

As successful as his valve was, Eddy's hydrant, which he developed over a period of years, was even more famous. The earliest model contained one of the most important features—an improved operating rod threaded below the frost line to prevent flooding in case the standpipe broke. The one-piece design was later modified to a two-piece design, and the main valve was changed to close against the water pressure, unlike other hydrant valves. Another key feature was the ability to remove the drip rod and drip valve through the top of the hydrant using ordinary tools for quick removal of obstructions, all without removing the main valve or shutting off the water from the mainline.

George Eddy successfully managed the company for nearly thirty years before selling it to Thomas Knickerbacker and his son John in 1875. The company continued to operate for another seventy years even though the innovations pioneered by Eddy had been developed decades earlier. In 1945, the company was sold to the Clow Valve Company of Oskaloosa, Iowa. Despite the change in ownership, the Eddy brand name was left intact

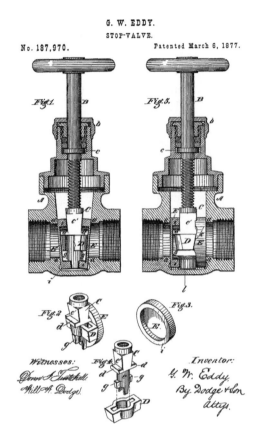

G. W. EDDY.
STOP-VALVE.
No. 187,970.
Patented March 6, 1877.

George Eddy's "Improvement in Stop-Valves."

by the parent company. Clow Valve still operates today and continues to manufacture the Eddy fire hydrant. Eddy passed away on December 5, 1897, at the age of eighty-six.

HENRY LUDLOW, TROY

Straight-Way Slide-Stop Valve

Some may find it hard to believe that an item such as a valve could support an entire industry, but the Eddy and Ludlow Valves sustained some of the largest and longest-lived businesses in the Troy-Waterford area. In fact, the Ludlow Valve, which went into production in 1861, is still being manufactured today, 150 years later.

Interior view of the Ludlow Valve Manufacturing Company. *Courtesy of the Library of Congress.*

The valve's inventor and namesake was Henry Gilbert Ludlow, born on March 28, 1823, in Nassau, New York. He graduated from Union College in Schenectady with an engineering degree and found employment as a gas engineer. His work in this field exposed him to valves and the shortcomings of those on the market. In 1861, he invented the Ludlow Straight-Way Sliding Stop Valve and, a few years later, decided to establish a company to manufacture it. He began in a small brick building on Second Street in Waterford, later moving to River Street and Vail Avenue in Troy. The Ludlow Valve Manufacturing Company was incorporated in 1866.

Although Ludlow's original valve was designed for gas pipes, it could also be used to control the flow of water. The uniqueness of the valve came from the use of two bevel-faced wedges held between the gates. As the stem was turned by hand, the upper wedge pressed against the lower one, forcing the gates tightly against their seats. When the valve was opened, the first turn of the stem moved the upper wedge out of contact with the lower one, releasing both gates from their seats. This eliminated the grinding and friction on the face bearing of the gates to greatly extend the life of the valve. Ludlow's hydrant later had the same feature, which figured prominently in its success.

The company expanded rapidly after moving to Lansingburgh in 1872 and offered a product line that included a variety of valves (gas, water, steam and oil), hydrants (yard, wash and fire) and other apparatus invented by Ludlow and others. Next, Ludlow moved the company to Troy and purchased the former Rensselaer Iron Company foundry building on the Poestenkill River. The factory buildings were not only larger but also had the added advantage of river and railroad transportation facilities nearby.

The Ludlow Valve became so well known that it almost became a genericized trademark. When the original patents began to expire, the

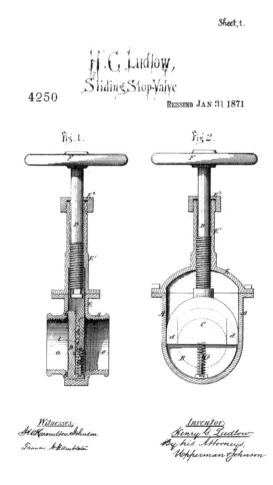

Henry Ludlow's "Improvement in Sliding Stop-Valves."

Pittsburgh Manufacturing Company (PMC) began making valves of Ludlow's design and prominently advertised them as "Ludlow Valves," with the actual name and location of PMC in small type at the bottom of the page. The company argued that the Ludlow name was so well known that it had become ubiquitous and therefore could not be trademarked. Ludlow sued and eventually forced PMC to stop using his name.

Ludlow filed over a dozen patents relating to valves, hydrants and various improvements. Some were more successful than others. For example, his Balanced Valve Hydrant had an ingenious design but was much more expensive than the designs of the competition. Conversely, Ludlow's Slide-Gate Valves were more economical and very reliable. The superior design of his valves and hydrants, combined with an aggressive sales policy, eventually resulted in the Ludlow Manufacturing Company becoming the largest valve manufacturer in the world.

After Ludlow retired from the business in the early 1890s, John Christie and his son-in-law James Caldwell assumed ownership. For many years, the company survived poor management, resistant labor unions, economic downturns and supply disadvantages. In 1954, the Ludlow firm merged with the Rensselaer Valve Company in Cohoes in an effort to remain viable but finally closed down in 1968. However, the Ludlow name lives on in the product line of the Patterson Pump Company of Georgia, which offers "Ludlow Rensselaer Low Pressure Gate Valves" that still use the double-wedge principle invented by Henry Ludlow.

JAMES KNIBBS, TROY

The Knibbs Run Around

Unless an inventor is careful in deciding when and in what way an invention is patented, the danger of infringement is greatly increased, and court fights to protect the invention can easily become costly and time-consuming. A perfect example of this calamity is the case of James Knibbs and his fire engine relief valve, otherwise known as the "Knibbs Run Around."

Knibbs was born on October 14, 1827, in Somerton, England. At the age of thirteen, his family immigrated to New York and settled in Troy, where Knibbs learned the machinist trade at the shop of Starbuck Brothers. In 1859, Knibbs perfected an important pressure valve for steam fire engines. Until that time, there was no effective method for using more than one hose on each fire engine without wasting water and subjecting the operators to the risk of injury. The danger would arise when one hose was shut off and the excess water was then diverted to the remaining open hoses. If two or more hoses were shut off, the full force of water would flow into the remaining hose, which sometimes burst from the pressure.

The Knibbs Run Around relief valve solved this problem by diverting the extra pressure to the receiving side of the pump. This meant that the pressure within the pump was the same whether one hose was in use or four. As an experiment, Knibbs had the valve manufactured and placed on a steamer for Troy's Arba Read Steam Fire Engine Company. In a series of tests, the valve not only made it safer to operate different numbers of hoses, but each stream of water was more powerful than the water streams of other engines. The fire company then appointed Knibbs as the first full-time steam engineer in the city of Troy and paid him the respectable sum of fifty dollars per month. According to the *Troy Times*, Knibbs and his steamer helped check the flames of the great Troy fire of 1862, which rapidly burned five hundred buildings.

In applying his valve to practical use, Knibbs made a grievous error. Rather than patent his invention first, he gave the specifications to the Amoskeag Manufacturing Company of New Hampshire so that it could install the device on the Arba Read engine. Amoskeag found that fire engines with the Knibbs valve installed performed so much better than those without the device that, unknown to Knibbs, the company immediately began installing the valve on every engine it produced. Since there was no patent to protect the device, municipalities and fire companies around the Northeast began to adopt the design into their fire engines. Curiously, this arrangement went on for about two years before Knibbs finally applied for a patent in 1864.

To complicate matters, Knibbs licensed a portion of the patent rights to Marcus Norton, who began a series of lawsuits against those who used the valve. One of the most public of these lawsuits was against the City of Boston. Norton asked for $450,000 in damages but lost when the city proved that it had been purchasing Amoskeag fire engines before the patent was issued. After that defeat, the patent rights were sold and resold to a string of investors until finally ending with Christopher Campbell of East Chatham, New York. Campbell commenced a million-dollar lawsuit against the City of New York. Since Knibbs retained a portion of the rights to his patent, he also filed a series of lawsuits. These court cases eventually expanded to include over five hundred cities around the country.

The lawsuits did not end after Knibbs's death on April 16, 1901. His heirs, as well as the heirs of Campbell's estate, continued the fight with

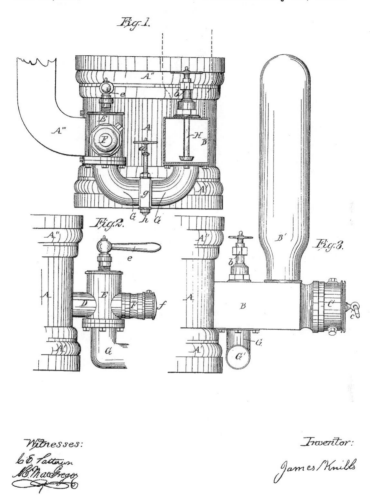

J. KNIBB.
PUMP.

No. 42,920.   Patented May 24, 1864.

Fig. 1.

Fig. 2.   *Fig. 3.*

Witnesses:

Inventor:
James Knibbs

James Knibbs's "Improvement in Pumps."

millions of dollars at stake, which was widely publicized around the country. Those municipalities that chose to fight, such as Boston and New York City, prevailed, while others chose to settle out of court. When the lawsuits finally ended, they together constituted one of the largest patent fights in United States history.

MEN OF STEEL

The manufacture of steel boils down to controlling the carbon content of iron. Iron ore must be infused with a specific quantity of carbon in order to be classified as steel. Iron with a carbon content lower than steel is known as wrought iron, while a higher carbon content turns the metal into cast, or pig, iron. Some steel was made prior to the 1800s by trial and error, but those early ironworkers did not realize that the level of carbon infused with iron determined what type of metal it would become.

The Capital District's iron and steel industry was at one time a significant employer in New York State but was slow to develop compared to those of other states. Ironworks had been established in Massachusetts, New Jersey, Pennsylvania and other Mid-Atlantic states by 1700, yet a century later, New York's iron industry was still undeveloped, for several reasons. The Dutch fur traders who first settled the area were reluctant to allow any other industrial development, fearing that their own interests would suffer. When the fur trade began to subside, the introduction of the manorial system, in which settlers leased farms from large land owners (known as the patroons), stifled large-scale settlement. Since the iron industry was labor-intensive, the small population was unable to adequately support any sizeable foundries.

It wasn't until the manorial system broke down that large-scale industry of any kind could take hold in the Hudson-Mohawk Valley. Beginning in 1800, a series of events led to the establishment and rapid growth of iron factories. Large concentrations of iron ore deposits were discovered in the Adirondacks and various points along the Hudson River Valley, including near Troy and Albany. Sand that was perfect for use in creating molds was

Men of Steel

Close-up view of the USS *Monitor* and its crew. The armor plating for the ship was fabricated at the foundry of John Winslow. Winslow also financed the ship's construction and was the actual owner during its famous battle with the *Merrimac*. *Courtesy of the Library of Congress.*

found in abundance near the Mohawk River, while seemingly limitless forests to provide fuel were close at hand.

Isaiah and John Townsend established the first Albany ironworks in 1807 that soon became known as the famous Townsend Furnace. An influx of settlers from New England arrived with knowledge of the industry and quickly set up more furnaces so that, by 1835, there were twenty ironworks operating in the Capital District. Much of the raw material was brought in from the Adirondacks along the new Champlain and Erie Canals, refined into iron and steel and then sent down the Hudson River to customers in New York City and beyond.

With the arrival of industrialists such as Erastus Corning, John Winslow and Henry Burden, the industry was expanded to such an extent that New York became one of the top iron-producing states. Winslow, along with Alexander Holly, purchased the rights to the Bessemer steel process of converting pig iron to steel and established the country's first Bessemer steel factory. Winslow also became known for helping to build the USS *Monitor* ironclad. Burden invented a horseshoe-making machine that was able to provide enough horseshoes to outfit the horses of almost the entire Union army during the Civil War.

While Henry Burden is the most famous inventor to come from the iron industry in this area, there were many others whose ideas were successfully turned into finished products. James Blessing's steam trap was so effective and innovative that a successful business was built to manufacture it. However, the original "Man of Steel," Horatio Gates Spafford, never manufactured steel or changed history with his innovations, even though there is evidence that he conjured up a process for making inexpensive steel before Henry Bessemer did.

HORATIO SPAFFORD, ALBANY

Iron and Steel Manufacture

It is well known that John Griswold and John Winslow of Troy purchased the American patents of England's Henry Bessemer in 1862 and built the first factory in America that produced Bessemer steel. However, there is evidence to suggest that an Albany resident named Horatio Gates Spafford invented a process for making inexpensive steel using oxygen decades earlier that was remarkably similar to that of Bessemer.

Spafford was born in Tinmouth, Vermont, on February 18, 1778, to a prominent military family. Although Spafford's father would have preferred that he follow the family tradition, Spafford was much more interested in science and literature. He taught school for a few years and, about 1800, began experimenting with light and heat. His first patent was filed in 1805 while he was living in Hudson, New York. His improvement in fireplaces was only the 599th patent filed in the United States. Nine years later, he patented an improvement in wheel carriages that featured a U-shaped axle fitted with an air bladder that acted as a cushion rather than springs.

Although his axle patent seems to give credence to the rumors that Spafford was a bit eccentric, General Stephen Van Rensselaer wrote in a letter, "If you converse with Spafford for half an hour you will perceive that his mind is stored with a great deal of knowledge original and acquired and there is no possible pretense for supposing that he is deranged." Spafford authored *A General Geography and Rudiments of Useful Knowledge* in 1809 and, four years later, published his famous *Gazetteer of the State of New York*, which today still serves as a useful reference for historians. For two years he published *American Magazine*, which circulated around Albany, and he also wrote a novel called *The Memoirs of Madam de Morville*. These publications as well as his scientific researches brought him in close contact with nearly all of the prominent men of the time, including Thomas Jefferson, James Madison and John Adams.

One of Spafford's lines of experiments involved manufacturing iron and steel. In 1816, he submitted an essay to be read before the American Philosophical Society titled "Cursory Observations on the Art of Making Iron and Steel from Native Ores of the United States." The manuscript allegedly described Spafford's ideas for infusing oxygen into iron ore in order to manufacture a type of steel less expensively than any other method.

The essay itself has been lost, but circumstantial evidence of its contents would lead one to believe that if Spafford had handled his invention differently, history would have recorded him as one of the world's greatest inventors. A committee of the society was formed to study Spafford's ideas but concluded that he left out too much detail for experiments to be performed. After four months had lapsed without word from the society, Spafford impatiently asked for the manuscript to be returned, fearing that his ideas would be exploited by others.

Fortunately, the letter that accompanied Spafford's manuscript still exists. An anonymous member of the society wrote, "Mr. Spafford's paper contains an idea which is both new and important. During the roasting of iron ores, first for the purpose of desulphurization, the next purpose should not be to take away but to add oxygen to the maximum. In this state, it is more fusible, requires less charcoal, and can be sooner freed from impurities." However, the writer went on to say that the manuscript was much too long to be properly understood yet left out crucial details in an effort to "throw an air of concealment" over the specifications.

Spafford's fear of copyright infringement did not end even after submitting two patents for "the art of making cast iron or steel" in 1822. Even though the government allowed the patents to be recorded, the same crucial details of how his process worked were omitted. The patents themselves were lost to the Patent Office fire of 1836, but identical letters that Spafford wrote to James Madison and Thomas Jefferson allude to the "concealment." He wrote, "I have realized the truth of a theory of great importance to the arts and to the country. How shall I avail myself of the benefit of this discovery? I ask thy advice. The system is all new and perfectly succeeds. I can make the very best cast steel from our native ores at about the expense of making refined bar iron." He then asked if he could apply to Congress for a special law to give the secretary of state the specifications of his steel patents under seal. If this law could be passed, he proposed, he would only ask for $5,000 per year for the life of the patent and that all iron and steel made from his process would be stamped "Spafford Steel" or "Spafford Ore."

Madison sent a letter of reply in which he doubted that Congress had the authority to create such a law. Although there is at least one letter from Jefferson to Spafford still in existence to prove the two were frequent correspondents, there is no record that he responded to this particular letter. Curiously, Spafford sent the full specifications of his experiments to Emperor Alexander of Russia through the Russian minister to the United States. The minister assured Spafford that "the secrecy of your invention will be strictly preserved."

Throughout much of his life, Spafford moved from place to place. Three of his five patents were filed in Albany, while one was filed in Troy and the other in Hudson. In 1811, Spafford purchased some land in Onondaga County, intending to settle there. He offered to furnish a library to the town if it received his name. The library was established, and the town was incorporated under the name "Spafford," but for some reason he decided to remain in the Capital region. Later, he moved briefly to Venango, Pennsylvania, where he started an experimental farm called Spafford's Settlement, but this venture failed, and he moved to Ballston Spa in 1816. Four years later, he was back in Albany to submit his iron and steel patents as well as a patent for making edge tools. None of these was replaced after being destroyed in 1836.

In late 1831, Spafford again petitioned Congress to grant him patent protection under a special provision to keep the specifications secret. This time it was for "a valuable discovery in natural and mechanical philosophy" that was supposed to double the power of any water source for mills. It was also asserted that the new machinery could be installed on oceangoing ships to provide power with "no expense for fuel." Several friends and acquaintances wrote testimonials to Congress in support of Spafford's mysterious invention. Elijah Willey of Lansingburgh wrote, in part, "This discovery embraces a new principle of mechanical power, and in its full development is of more importance to the interests and honor of the country than any discovery since we were a nation." Spafford needed a formal patent so that he could sell part of the interest in it, since he had spent all of his money in developing this and other inventions. However, before Congress could act on his request, he passed away on August 7, 1832, and a patent was never awarded.

It is indeed unfortunate that Spafford's obsession with secrecy denied the world his theories for water power as well as manufacturing cast steel. It wouldn't be until Sir Henry Bessemer read his famous paper to the British Association for the Advancement of Science some forty years later that the process of making steel would make that important step forward. The only hope for a revision of history, which fades every year, is that either the original patent awarded to Spafford survives in someone's collection or that the specifications sent to Emperor Alexander will someday be found at the Kremlin.

HENRY BURDEN, TROY

Horseshoe Machine

The number of patents Henry Burden was awarded was small compared to other notable inventors in the region, but each was among the most important in the history of the industrial arts. The success of his inventions directly correlated to the growth of his mammoth foundry and its achievement as a company of national importance, especially during the Civil War.

Burden was born in Dunblane, Scotland, on April 22, 1791, and showed a remarkable aptitude for invention at an early age while working on his father's farm. His mind was constantly devising labor-saving devices using the most basic materials. His first successful invention was a threshing machine for separating grain from the stalks and husks. After attending the school of mathematician William Hawley, Burden was determined to immigrate to America to seek his fortune as an engineer and inventor.

After arriving in Albany in 1819, Burden continued to construct new agricultural implements. His first creation was an improved plow that took first prize at several county fairs. Encouraged by this, he invented one of the country's first practical cultivators. Thereafter, he began patenting his inventions to protect his ideas, the first being a hemp and flax machine in 1822. That same year, he relocated from Albany to South Troy and became a selling agent for the Troy Iron and Nail Factory, which at the time was a small business with a capital of $96,000. The mill contained a single pair of rollers powered by two water wheels. Burden would devote the next forty years of his life to the mill's development and growth.

Most inventors with multiple patents are lucky if only one or two are successful. Burden's patent portfolio is all the more impressive because most of his patents were put to use in his foundry, and a few were among the most important patents of his time. For example, he developed a

Henry Burden
(1791–1871). *Courtesy*
of the Library of
Congress.

machine for making wrought-iron nails and spikes. At first, shipbuilders were against the new machine, as they thought it could not possibly manufacture spikes as good as could be made by hand. As railroads began to be constructed around the country and the demand for spikes skyrocketed, this prejudice evaporated.

In 1835, Burden traveled to Europe and decided that the flat rail was about to be superseded by the "T" rail that is used today, so he patented an improvement in his machine that would make spikes particularly suited to holding down the new rail (called the "hook-headed" spike). His first contract was with the Long Island Railroad Company, which ordered ten tons of his improved spikes. The owners of the Troy Iron Works paid Burden 30 percent of the entire company's net earnings in exchange for the rights to his patent. The spike was so successful that several manufacturers copied the design. Burden was forced to protect his patent from these manufacturers, including his neighbor, the famous railroad tycoon and iron manufacturer Erastus Corning. This resulted in the most protracted and costly lawsuit in history until that time, lasting thirteen years and involving some of the most prominent lawyers in the country, including Daniel Webster.

A few years after perfecting his spike machine, Burden constructed what was at the time the most famous water wheel in the world. Called the "Niagara of water wheels," it was an overshot wheel measuring sixty feet in diameter and twenty-two feet wide that generated up to 700 horsepower. The first wheel was later replaced by a second, larger wheel that allegedly generated 1,200 horsepower.

While he was constructing his famous water wheel, Burden came up with the idea of revolving puddle balls between concentric surfaces. Puddling was the process by which pig iron and steel were changed from melted, globular forms into cylindrical shapes. Burden's "Rotary Concentric Squeezer" was revolutionary in its day, resulting in a dramatic decrease in the production cost of converting puddle balls to wrought iron. The commissioner of patents declared that it was the "first truly original and most important invention in the manufacture of iron that has yet been submitted." When Burden submitted the patent on the machine to be renewed for an additional seven years, several iron men from Pittsburgh testified that during the short time they used his machine it had saved them over half a million dollars each.

The great importance of Burden's other inventions nearly paled in comparison to his famous horseshoe machine. Refined over a period of years, he finally submitted a patent for it in 1835. The original machine was able to manufacture a horseshoe in only two movements, but in 1857 he perfected a machine that accepted a heated bar and cut, bent and forged it into a horseshoe with only one movement.

The machine was a marvel of ingenuity. Company records describe how one of them was sent to the Austrian government for a demonstration. Curiosity of the new contraption spread, and guards had to be called to keep the crowds away while it was being assembled. When the machine was started, it began throwing out horseshoes faster than anyone could count. The crowd believed that it was a supernatural monster and fled the scene in wild confusion.

The American government was quite interested in the new invention, mindful of horseshoe shortages during the Mexican War. When the Civil War broke out, Burden's machine supplied the Union armies with nearly all of their horseshoes. Many wondered how the North could have effectively fought on horseback without the machine. The Southern armies were forced to rely on Burden horseshoes that came to them through depots and trains captured from the enemy. As the Confederacy's successes dwindled, it was forced to take action. A spy was sent to steal a copy of Burden's pattern

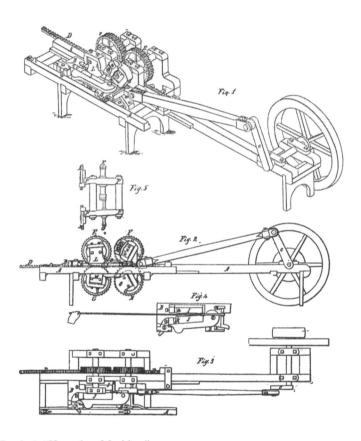

Henry Burden's "Horseshoe Machine."

and smuggle it to Canada. Fortunately for the North, General Sherman's advance through the Southern states foiled the plan.

As a direct result of Burden's inventions, the Troy Iron and Nail Factory steadily grew to become an immense industrial complex. Burden gradually purchased more and more stock in the company until he was the sole owner. The name was changed to the Burden Iron Works, later called H. Burden and Sons when his sons James and Townsend were admitted. Little trace of the original mill remained by that time. In its place were two huge sections built in 1862, called the Upper Works and the Lower Works. The Upper Works, located on the Wynantskill and powered by his famous water wheel, consisted of a fifty-thousand-square-foot rolling mill and puddling forge, a horseshoe factory, a rivet factory and a horseshoe warehouse capable of storing seven thousand tons. The Lower Works, located on the banks of the Hudson River and powered by steam, consisted of two blast furnaces, a forty-thousand-square-foot puddling forge, a forty-thousand-square-foot rolling mill, a foundry and various swaging, punching, machine and pattern shops.

The property had a significant river frontage convenient to the Hudson River Railroad. The river was dredged so that large vessels could tie up near the shops and be loaded with finished goods. In all, the shops contained sixty puddling furnaces, twelve rivet machines, three of Burden's rotary concentric squeezers and nine of his horseshoe machines. The horseshoe machines alone were capable of manufacturing fifty-one million horseshoes per year, enough to shod twelve million horses. These found a market in every part of North America and annually generated $2 million in revenue. At its height, Burden's labor-intensive works employed three thousand men, directly or indirectly supporting one-eighth of the population of Troy.

Burden passed away of heart disease on January 19, 1871, leaving behind two sons and three daughters. It is unfortunate that most of his earliest patents were destroyed in the Patent Office fire of 1836 (and perplexing that Burden did not provide replacements). His great water wheel served the works for fifty years before being abandoned in 1890. It remained on display outdoors as a reminder of a more prosperous and exciting age before it collapsed twenty years later. Republic Steel purchased the Burden property and manufactured iron at the site before closing down in 1972. The former office building of the Burden Iron Works now contains a museum operated by the Hudson Mohawk Industrial Gateway.

JOHN WINSLOW, TROY

Armor Plating

The naval battle between the ironclads *Monitor* and *Merrimac* in March 1862 was not only one of the most famous incidents of the Civil War, but it also changed naval warfare forever as navies around the world began to convert their wooden ships to ships made of steel. The Capital District was rightly proud of the *Monitor*'s performance in the battle, as the ship had intimate connections with the area. The Clute Brothers Foundry in Schenectady built the steam engine that powered the revolving gun turret, Saratoga Springs resident Theodore Timby invented the turret itself, and the Rensselaer Iron Works of Troy cast the iron plating. John Flack Winslow, one of Rensselaer Iron's proprietors, devised the iron plating as well as almost single-handedly financed the ship's construction and actually owned it at the time of the famous battle.

Winslow was born in Bennington, Vermont on November 10, 1810, and was a direct descendant of Kenelm Winslow, whose brother Edward Winslow was a *Mayflower* colonist and governor of Plymouth Colony. At the age of twenty-one, John Winslow became an agent for the New Jersey Iron Company at the Boston office, where he gained valuable administrative experience in the manufacture of iron and steel. Two years later, he established a small foundry in New Jersey for making pig iron.

He decided to relocate to Troy in 1837, where the greatest potential for manufacturing iron and steel existed. Winslow formed a partnership with Erastus Corning and James Horner, who were operating a foundry that produced iron nails. The foundry grew rapidly in size over the next two decades, consisting of the Albany Iron Works, the Bessemer Steel Works, the Troy Steel and Iron Company and the Rensselaer Iron Works, all located in and around Troy. Although Winslow was part owner of all of these divisions, he had primary charge of the Albany Iron Works, located on the Wynantskill River. The first "puddling," or producing wrought iron from pig iron, was introduced at this factory one year after Winslow arrived, making it only the second of its kind in the country.

In September 1861, as the Civil War neared, John Winslow and John Griswold traveled to Washington, D.C., to collect money due to the company for armor plating used to retrofit the wooden warship *Galena*. While there, they met Swedish engineer John Ericsson, who was attempting to submit plans for building a warship made entirely of steel and armed with a revolving gun battery. He showed his plans to Winslow and Griswold, who were impressed with the design and agreed to help him lobby the government for a contract.

Using Winslow's affiliation with Secretary of State John Seward, the three managed to obtain an audience with President Lincoln himself. After hearing their proposal, Lincoln set up a meeting with Commodore Smith the following morning. Winslow presented the plan once again to the president, the secretary of the navy and several other government officials. Lincoln

John Winslow (1810–1892). *Rensselaer County Historical Society collection.*

stated, "I think there is something in it, as the girl said when she put her foot in the stocking."

Although all present seemed to be in favor of constructing such a warship, the best Winslow could obtain was a verbal order from Secretary Welles and a Congressional board to begin construction. Griswold and Winslow decided to begin building the ship without waiting for a signed contract, knowing that it would take several months to complete and every day would be critical if war broke out. John Winslow wrote a letter to Ericsson within days of their Washington visit, which read in part, "Allow me to ask that you give me your specification for the plates for the lower boat at your earliest convenience, as I want to prepare the slabs in readiness for rolling. I shall make these hull plates of scrap iron, greatly superior in strength and purity compared to the ordinary puddle ship-plates."

On October 4, the contract was signed, and Winslow set a deadline of one hundred days to complete the world's first iron warship. As work progressed, he submitted a patent for improved armor plating to protect the innovations that were being used to build the historic ship. His patent consisted of "the construction, interlacing, and interlocking plates or bars for armor for warships so that the same shall be protected from injury by bombs or balls thrown from cannon battery and at the same time be of light draft of water, the said armor plates being securely fastened to the sides of such ships without exposing the heads of the fastening bolts to the outside surface of said armor plate."

The USS *Monitor* was launched exactly 101 working days after construction began. On March 9, it engaged the Confederate ship *Merrimac* near Hampton Roads, Virginia. The two ships exchanged fire for hours, but neither could pierce the armor of the other. Militarily, the battle was considered a draw, but the *Monitor* successfully stopped the *Merrimac* from continuing on its fearsome quest to sink Union warships at will.

Although it was well known at the time, few today know that the *Monitor* was not technically owned by the federal government at the time of its famous battle. The navy released payments for the vessel as construction progressed, but by contract agreement, 25 percent of the final bill would be withheld until the secretary of state was satisfied with its performance. Since there was no time to test the vessel, its trial run consisted of the actual battle with the *Merrimac*. Therefore, title to the vessel belonged to John Winslow, who had arranged to finance the $275,000 cost personally. The final payment of $68,750 was made five days after the battle, at which time Winslow was called "the benefactor of the nation" by many newspapers. The government almost immediately awarded the Albany Iron Works contracts to build more ironclads.

Winslow was a prolific inventor who submitted a variety of patents during his working career. His most important was for the armor plating noted above, but he also submitted a patent years earlier in 1852 for manufacturing railroad chairs (used for fastening rails together). During the war, a large number of his solid lip railroad chairs were used on military railroads constructed by the Union army as it advanced south through Virginia, Georgia, Kentucky

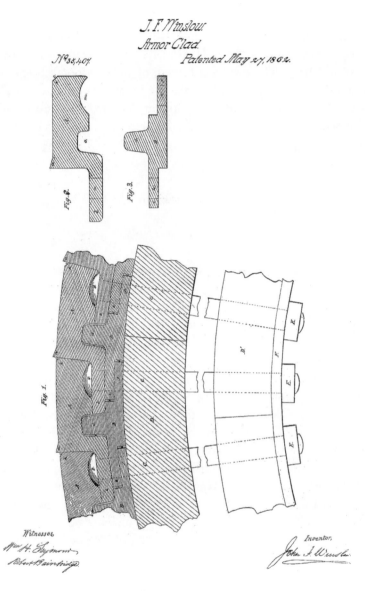

John Winslow's "Improved Armor-Plate for Vessels."

and Tennessee. Other patents dating back to 1843 included machines for puddling iron balls, a horseshoe machine, a machine for welding iron pipes and a machine for making hook- or brad-headed spikes.

The Rensselaer Polytechnic Institute appointed Winslow as its president in 1865, a position he held for three years. He retired from the foundry business and moved to Poughkeepsie, where he purchased a thirty-five-room mansion on the Hudson River. He passed away on March 10, 1892, and was buried in Albany, where he spent much of his childhood. Some historians contend that if Winslow did not take the initiative to finance and build the *Monitor*, the *Merrimac* would have gone on to destroy the entire Union navy and the conflict would have taken a different turn, perhaps lengthening the Civil War by a period of years.

JAMES BLESSING, ALBANY

Steam Trap

Heating buildings with steam was a vast improvement over stoves, especially for heating large office buildings or factories where a number of stoves would have been required. An early problem with steam heating units was the buildup of condensation within the machinery and a loss of pressure in the boiler. Various attempts were made to capture the condensation and return it to the boiler while maintaining the internal pressure, but none succeeded until James Blessing invented his famous and widely used steam trap.

Blessing was born in French's Mills, Albany County, on September 14, 1837. Upon the death of his father in 1849, he left school and became apprenticed in the machine shop of John Townsend. Townsend and his brother Isaiah owned the famous Townsend Furnace, one of the area's first foundries, which manufactured machine castings and railroad car wheels. At the outbreak of the Civil War, Blessing joined the U.S. navy and served as an assistant engineer. After the war, he was hired as chief engineer of the Brooklyn Horse Railroad Company for a few years before returning to Albany and joining the firm of Townsend and Jackson, which was headed by John Townsend's nephew Franklin.

In 1870, Townsend decided to relocate the foundry closer to the Hudson River in a new, four-story brick building. Blessing was charged with the task of devising a heating system for the new factory. The idea for his steam trap came to him when he realized a mistake had been made in configuring the heater. He had placed the boiler in a pit so that the condensation from the entire building would gravitate to it. However, the pit was located so low that the Hudson River would sometimes rise above the boiler's firebox. Rather than reconfigure the entire system, Blessing experimented with a spherical vessel that acted as a condensation receiver near the boiler. Pipes were then

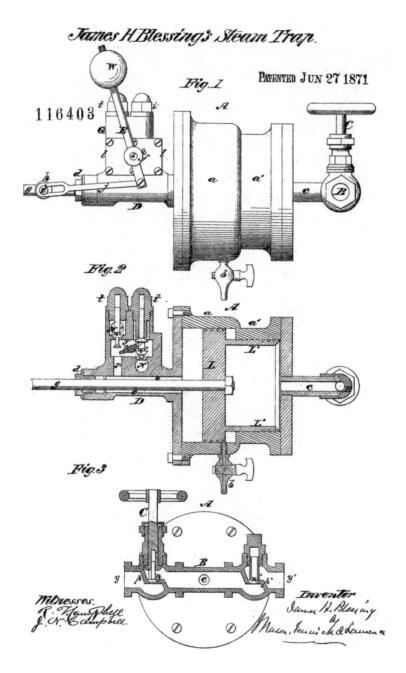

James Blessing's "Improvement in Steam Traps."

inserted from the radiators to the vessel and from the vessel to the boiler. This arrangement constituted the first steam loop ever devised that returned condensation from a steam system situated below the water level of the boiler, as well as the first to deliver steam without opening to the atmosphere.

He further developed the steam loop, which relied on long pipes to equalize the pressure between the boiler and its steam system, and the steam trap, which used steam from the boiler to achieve equal pressure. Blessing was awarded a series of patents for his devices beginning in 1871. Dozens of other patents were awarded for different types of heating systems, water purification systems and a wide variety of component parts, such as boilers, pumps, drains, valves, pump governors and friction clutches.

Within a year of perfecting his steam trap, Blessing started his own company on Church Street in Albany with business partner General Frederick Townsend. The firm's sole purpose was to manufacture Blessing's steam traps and other devices that he invented. The business was a success, and the Albany Steam Trap Company was incorporated in 1875 with three stockholders: General Townsend, Henry Martin and Blessing, who acted as secretary, treasurer and superintendent.

Over the following decades, Blessing's steam traps came into wide use around the country as steam was increasingly used to heat buildings and manufacture goods, such as in paper mills and refineries. Besides operating his successful business, Blessing was elected mayor of Albany in 1899 and served one term, declining further offices due to poor health. He passed away on February 21, 1910, as one of Albany's most successful inventors.

THE COLLAR CITY

The term "Collar City" is well known in the Capital District, although not everyone knows its significance. The collar and shirt industry originated in Troy and for years was one of the region's greatest employers, giving jobs to thousands of men and women for decades.

It all began in 1827, when a woman named Hannah Lord Montague decided that she was tired of washing her husband's shirts when only the collar was dirty. As an experiment, she cut off one of his collars, washed it and sewed it back onto the shirt. When Mr. Montague seemed agreeable to the idea of separating all of the collars from his shirts, Hannah realized that easily detachable collars could be the answer that many overworked wives were seeking.

As news of Hannah's idea spread throughout the city, retired Methodist minister Ebenezer Brown set up a small collar-making operation at his shop on River Street with his wife and daughter. There they began manufacturing the world's first detachable collars, consisting of a two-ply material that had to be taped and tied to the shirt. Brown sold his so-called "string collars" door to door for twenty-five cents each.

Hannah's husband, Orlando, also got in on the act and partnered with Austin Granger to manufacture "string" and "Bishop" collars at 222 River Street. The following year, Lyman Bennett created a system in which his wife would cut the cloth into shapes and bring them to workers' homes for stitching, starching and ironing. The finished collars were delivered to customers in wagons called the "collar express." A man named Independence Starks opened a collar and cuff shop at 66 North Second Street in 1835.

Later, he added the city's first laundry, where he washed not only his own collars but those of his competitors as well, establishing a new industry.

The famous Wheeler sewing machines were introduced to Troy in 1852 by Wheeler, Wilson and Company. Troy resident Jefferson Gardner was the first person to utilize the new Wheeler machines, which greatly increased production capacity. The sewing machine also created skilled workers, so that many women were able to earn more in one day than they had previously in an entire week.

Over the next two decades, the various technologies for mass-producing millions of collars, cuffs and shirts were developed by local inventors. Dozens of patents were filed for collar and shirt designs, improvements in production processes and new machinery. Many of these patents were filed by collar factory owners and were applied directly to the manufacturing process.

By 1900, there were approximately twenty-six collar and cuff manufacturers that employed some fifteen thousand people. Ninety percent of all collars in America were made in Troy, as name brands such as Arrow and Lion became known around the world. Sanford Cluett's preshrinking fabric machine changed the way shirts were made and, for the first time, gave consumers confidence in the stated size of their clothing. He is also one of the few inventors whose innovation is still licensed and used to this day.

Although most collar manufacturers had either closed or moved south by the 1950s, it was remarkable that an industry that started out so inconspicuously endured for more than a century as one of the area's greatest employers. Beginning with Hannah Montague's invention of the detachable collar to the hundreds of inventions that followed, the patents that made Troy the Collar City are among the most important in the Capital District.

SANFORD CLUETT, TROY

Preshrinking Cotton Fabrics

There was a time when the size indicated on a shirt label would not necessarily be the same when it emerged from its first laundering. Most people purchased shirts and collars one size too big in the hopes that they would shrink to fit properly. The invention of Sanford Lockwood Cluett solved this problem and changed the manufacture of shirts in a way that few other inventions did.

Sanford Cluett
(1874–1968). *Courtesy
of the Folsom Library,
Rensselaer Polytechnic
Institute.*

Cluett was born in 1874 to Edmund and Mary Alice Cluett of Troy. Edmund's brothers included John, George and Robert, who established the firm that would later become Cluett, Peabody and Company. Sanford displayed an inquisitive mind from an early age. When he was ten years old, he surveyed and mapped Raquette Lake in the Adirondacks using a carpenter's level, some screw eyes and a music stand. He lived in Florida during his teen years, befriending the Seminole Indians and learning their language.

Upon returning to Troy, he attended the Troy Academy and graduated in 1894. Four years later, he obtained a degree in civil engineering from Rensselaer Polytechnic Institute, where he researched ballistics. He then joined the New York National Guard and participated in the Spanish-American War as a member of the New York Volunteer Infantry. He remained with the National Guard until 1917, retiring with the rank of major. In the meantime, he moved to Hoosick Falls and became at various times chief engineer, superintendent and vice-president of the Walter A. Wood Mowing and Reaping Company.

Cluett's first known invention was the Bubble Sextant for Celestial Navigation in 1896. While working for Walter Wood, he developed one-horse and two-horse mowers with an adjustable cutting bar operable from the driver's seat. Other inventions included an improved harrow-tooth clip, a valve gate and a mower "tilting lever quadrant" for controlling the tilt of the cutter bar.

In 1919, he decided to move back to Troy and join his uncles at Cluett, Peabody and Company. In that year, the firm enjoyed record revenues of $32 million, mainly from its wildly successful Arrow Collar. The advertising campaign for the collar centered on the Arrow Collar Man, created by artist Joseph Leyendecker. However, soon after that revenue milestone, sales plummeted as the buying public began to favor soft, collar-attached shirts. Company president Chesly Palmer decided to focus production solely on shirts in the 1930s, but sales remained lower than they had been in the early part of the century.

Luckily, Vice-president Sanford Cluett, the last executive of the original Cluett-Peabody families, was experimenting with a process for preshrinking fabrics. The public was becoming increasingly dissatisfied with clothing of a stated size that shrank after each wash until it often became too small to wear. Customers were unwilling to buy prewashed clothing, and no one could figure out how to shrink clothing without repeatedly washing it.

Scientists around the country attempted to solve the problem. After spending several years on the problem himself, Cluett was the first to find a viable solution. He discovered that shrinkage was caused as a result of the manufacturing process, as fabrics would be stretched as they were passed through the spinning, weaving and bleaching machinery. During the first wash, the fabric would simply "shrink" back to its normal state.

His first and most important patent related to shrinking fabric was awarded in 1929, in which the basic tenets of his theory were introduced to the world. It consisted of a machine that laterally stretched and longitudinally shrank a fabric web using an endless series of uniformly spaced "impaling" pins and elastic felt blanket. His 1932 improvement used a humidifying treatment to soften the fabric before being subjected to the longitudinal shrinking operation. A third patent combined the mechanisms and processes of the first two, involving a multistage shrinking operation that featured adjustable lengthwise and widthwise shrinking. A fourth improvement added a rotary drying and ironing cylinder. Cluett's process removed the tension in the yarn by eliminating the friction within the fabric. Water and soap were used as lubricant during the laundering process to "relax" the fibers and let them contract to their original length. Samples of each batch were wash-tested to determine the shrinkage of each before running the fabric through his machine.

The new process was an immediate success, and sales of the Arrow Shirt skyrocketed. The company also benefited from royalties by licensing the process and making it available to all clothing manufacturers. A 1948 *TIME* magazine article stated that total royalties amounted to $7 million, which equaled the total profit from the company's shirt sales. In honor of its inventor, the process became known as "Sanforizing" when the company registered it with the United States Patent and Trademark Office in 1930.

Other trademarks followed. A process that would become known as Sanforset guaranteed that rayon fabrics would not shrink or stretch more than 2 percent. Wool that had been treated to make it permanently non-

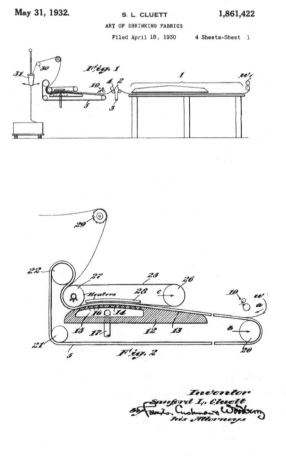

Sanford Cluett's "Art of Shrinking Fabrics."

felting was called Sanforian. Sanforized Plus and Sanforized Plus 2 indicated that the garments were certified to meet the company's strict standards for crease recovery, tensile strength and smoothness retention.

Another of Cluett's inventions was Clupak, a stretchable bag material that was difficult to tear. The West Virginia Pulp and Paper Company (which owned a giant paper mill in Mechanicville, New York) entered into an agreement with Cluett, Peabody and Company to further develop the paper and sell it to a worldwide market. The new paper became popular with companies that distributed heavy materials such as chemicals and cement, as well as shopping bags and wrapping paper.

Sanford Cluett's remarkable preshrinking idea not only ensured the long-term survival of Cluett, Peabody and Company, but it also revolutionized the way clothing was manufactured. When he died in 1968, his process was licensed by almost 450 mills in fifty-eight countries around the world. Even with the advent of modern technology, it is still licensed in one hundred countries today. Cluett was also one of the area's most prolific inventors, with over two hundred patents awarded over his lifetime.

HOWARD KENNEDY, TROY

Shirts and Collars

Hundreds of collar and shirt patents were filed in Troy, many of which were quietly implemented in factories throughout the city. The majority of these improvement and design patents did not receive any public notice but were the backbone of the collar industry and enabled Troy to maintain its place as the collar and shirt capital for as long as it did.

These types of "forgotten" patents were exemplified by Howard Samuel Kennedy, who worked in the collar industry for much of his life and eventually became president of Cluett, Peabody and Company. Kennedy was born on July 11, 1858, in Troy and educated in the public schools. As a boy, his first work experience was in the collar mill of Coon and Van Valkenburgh, which later became Coon and Company. After working there for a number of years, he was made superintendent of the factory.

In 1889, Coon and Company, which was the second-largest clothing manufacturer in the city at the time, consolidated with the largest collar manufacturer, that of George Cluett, Brothers and Company. Kennedy was made general manager of all the firm's factories and became a partner in

1899. When the firm was incorporated as Cluett, Peabody and Company two years later, he was appointed third vice-president. He then served as the company's president for three years beginning in 1916.

Kennedy was awarded a number of patents in the early 1900s, all assigned to Cluett, Peabody and Company. They were for minor improvements in the design or manufacture of shirts and collars and are indicative of the many that were filed in support of the industry. One patent described a method for facilitating the insertion of a stud or collar button in a wall of a shirt pocket. Another improvement made it easier to button and unbutton an open bosom dress shirt by using notches rather than buttonholes. Three patents related to improving the design of collars, such as a "turn-over" collar made with an inner band and downwardly turned top that was attached to the band. Yet another patent described a new process for bending down the points of a laundered "standing" collar to increase its durability.

Kennedy's son Richard followed in his father's footsteps, beginning his career as a shipping clerk at Cluett, Peabody and working his way up to the position of assistant to the vice-president. Richard was also awarded a number of patents for various types of collars, shirts and coats. These were more examples of minor improvements that enabled Cluett, Peabody to maintain a competitive edge over other manufacturers. One collar patent was for a reinforced band to resist the tendency of collars to wrinkle and become deformed. He also developed a reversible collar that could be detached, turned over and reattached when one side became worn out, without the need to manually create another buttonhole.

Howard Kennedy was also an example of a successful businessman who was active in the community. He dedicated each Sunday to teaching a class at the Trinity Methodist Episcopal Church called "Life Lights" that numbered 150 men. In addition, he was involved with the Young Men's Christian Association, the Law and Order League, the Social Union of Troy, the Poultney Academy, the Adirondack Spring Company and the Lancaster Realty Company. He passed away on January 23, 1938, at the age of eighty.

JAMES PINE, LANSINGBURGH

Collar and Cuff Machines

On May 7, 1890, the United Shirt and Collar Company came into being by consolidating five of Troy's most successful collar companies, making it

James K.P. Pine
(1841–1919).
*Rensselaer County
Historical Society
collection.*

the largest collar firm in the world. The man behind this deal was clothing manufacturer James Knox Polk Pine, who was also one of the most prolific inventors in the collar and cuff industry.

Pine was born in the Rensselaer County town of Hoosick on November 21, 1841, and educated at Ball's Academy in Hoosick Falls. His father, James Pine Sr., was employed by the Walter A. Wood Company, an agricultural implement manufacturer. He later established a small factory in Troy to produce several harvesters, mowing machines and a rope machine that he invented.

The younger James began his business career in 1860 as a clerk for the collar firm Coon and Van Valkenburg. Just two years later, he became an equal partner in the firm Cole, Dyer and Pine to manufacture collars. Pine retained his interests through several name and ownership changes until he was the senior partner of Pine and Hamblin in 1880. After Myron Hamblin died, he conducted the business alone and erected the huge Lion Factory building on Second Avenue.

J. K. P. PINE.
MACHINE FOR BENDING COLLARS AND THE LIKE.
APPLICATION FILED AUG. 18, 1905.

974,426.

Patented Nov. 1, 1910.

3 SHEETS—SHEET 1.

James Pine's "Machine for Bending Collars and the Like."

Beginning in 1875, Pine began devising and patenting dozens of inventions that related to the manufacture of collars, cuffs and clothing. Many were designs for "standing collars," shirts and undergarments. He also had great mechanical abilities, as evidenced by the invention of complex machinery for folding, stretching and manufacturing collars. One patent for a machine that folded the edges of collar and cuff blanks consisted of ten pages of highly technical drawings and descriptions.

Although the detachable collar was invented in Troy, by the 1880s the manufacture of collars and cuffs was widespread around the country. Pine and other Troy manufacturers sought a solution to the heightened competition and formed the United Shirt and Collar Company, capitalized at $2 million. It was made up of the James K.P. Pine Company, Beiermeister and Spicer, Sanford and Robinson, Marshall and Briggs and S.A. House's Sons. Pine, who was the single largest stockholder, was elected treasurer of the new organization, then named vice-president and finally president in 1906 upon the death of Samuel Sanford.

The original five companies retained their identities and trademarks after the United Shirt consolidation. Pine's mill was best known for its "Lion Brand" trademark, and he later renamed it Lion Collars and Shirts, Inc. He also owned the Troy Carriage Works on Third Avenue, where he manufactured carriages, wagons and sleighs. Several patents supported this business as well, such as a sleigh, wagon spring and improved harness. He was also active in the community, serving as president of the People's Bank of Lansingburgh, director of the Ostrander Fire Brick Company and a stockholder of the Record Publishing Company.

Due in part to cooperation among its collar mills, Troy was able to hold on to its dominance of the collar industry for decades despite intense competition from both domestic and foreign collar companies. In the early 1900s, the thirty factories in Troy still produced 90 percent of all collars and cuffs in the country. Pine remained president of the United Shirt and Collar Company until his death in Castleton, Vermont, on September 16, 1919. His last patent, the "Union Undergarment," which combined a shirt and drawers into one piece of clothing, was awarded just a few months before he died. The United Shirt and Collar Company did not survive very long after the death of its founder, dissolving in 1922.

THOMAS WILES, TROY

Ironing Machines

The success of the shirt and collar industry in Troy spawned several other significant industries that helped support it. The laundering business alone employed more than two thousand women in the late 1800s. The growth of laundering, in turn, created an ongoing need for the latest machinery, creating yet another industry.

As the inventor of several important washing and ironing machines, Thomas Squires Wiles was influential in the success of both the laundering and laundry machinery industries. He was born in Albany on September 28, 1838, and graduated from the Wesleyan University in Middletown, Connecticut. Returning home to the Capital District, he established the Wiles Laundering Company on William Street in Troy, laundering collars for nearby manufacturers on a small scale. A few years later, he expanded his operations by taking over the St. Nicholas Laundry and moved to a spacious building on Union Street. A second location was later established on Sixth Street.

The expansion of the business rested on Wiles's improved ironing machines, patented in 1873 and 1876. They were a vast improvement over the primitive machines of the time, using a series of heated metallic rollers. The rollers were covered in muslin or similar material to absorb and discharge the moisture from the cloth as it passed through the machine. An elastic covering beneath the muslin allowed a degree of yield for hems, seams or other thick parts of the clothing. The belts and pulleys were arranged so that each had time to cool as it revolved away from the clothing, allowing the machines to run continuously without overheating. In practice, each machine was able to iron over twelve thousand collars per day.

In addition to his famous ironing machines, Wiles patented a variety of related machinery that helped him expand his services. His improved clothes-drying frame was able to withstand extreme heat for much longer periods of time than the traditional wood-framed dryers. His improved wringer (known as a "mangle") was designed to help dry clothing without the usual side effects of hardening, compressing or otherwise damaging the material. He also developed a combined dampening and ironing machine, a machine for moistening the fold-lines of collars and a special cloth carrier that could be adapted to a variety of machines.

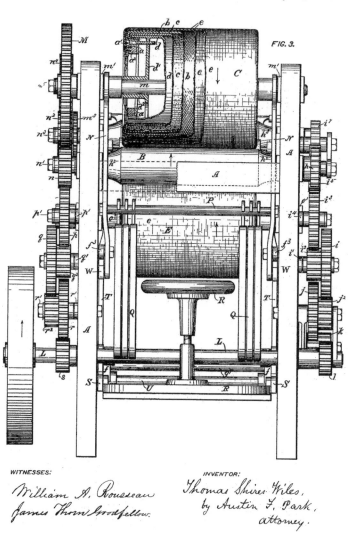

T. S. WILES.
IRONING APPARATUS.

No. 177,908.

Patented May 23, 1876.

FIG. 3.

WITNESSES:

William A. Rousseau
James Thorn Goodfellow.

INVENTOR:

Thomas Shirer Wiles,
by Austin F. Park,
attorney.

Thomas Wiles's "Improvement in Ironing Apparatus."

The Collar City

The Wiles Laundering Company quickly became the largest of its kind in the city, employing 250 women. Customers included most of the collar and shirt manufacturers in Troy as well as manufacturers outside of the city, since Wiles was able to launder clothing less expensively than others could. The machinery in each of the departments was designed to wash, dry, starch, dampen and iron shirts and collars by the millions per month.

In 1881, several area capitalists invested $150,000 to establish the Troy Laundry Manufacturing Company to manufacture Wiles's machinery. A factory was set up at 650 Fulton Street that employed about 150 men. A second factory was soon erected in Chicago, while salesrooms were established in New York, London and Berlin to handle the worldwide demand.

Wiles was one of the Capital District's great inventors, with dozens of patents awarded throughout his life. His passion outside of the laundry business was photography. He was secretary of the Albany Camera Club, and several of his patents related to improvements in that field, such as a magazine camera and a photographic plate developing tray. Three patents were for a telescopic stand pipe that could be set up by firemen next to a burning building to reach fires that were several floors above ground. Other patents included an improved mailbox, an improvement in gas-burning heaters, a necktie and a seamless felted fabric that could be used as a filter.

Even with the long list of clever and useful patents, Wiles will be remembered for the machinery that did so much to advance the shirt and collar industry of Troy. Without an inexpensive and efficient means to launder, iron and otherwise prepare their products for sale, Troy manufacturers could not have grown as fast or remained as profitable as they did for such a long period of time.

THE SPINDLE CITY

The city of Cohoes owes its historical prominence in the knitting industry to the waterfall located nearby on the Mohawk River, the second largest in the state after Niagara Falls. Although as early as 1811 the Cohoes Manufacturing Company was producing cotton, woolen and linen goods, it wasn't until Timothy Bailey invented the world's first power knitting machine twenty years later that Cohoes was set upon the path to become the Spindle City.

The first dam near Cohoes Falls that provided enough power for a substantial industrial center was constructed in 1831. In addition, a series of ten canals was constructed at various levels that drew water off the falls, powered machinery and then returned the water back to the Mohawk. Bailey and his business partner, Egbert Egberts, were attracted to Cohoes by the ample water power generated by these dams and canals.

While the knitting industry was still in its infancy in America, the Harmony Cotton Manufacturing Company was incorporated and acquired rights to the Cohoes Falls for power. This mill grew over the years to become the largest cotton mill in the world, containing an astonishing 275,000 spindles within 6,200 looms. Mill Number 3, known as the Mastodon Mill because the bones of a prehistoric mastodon were discovered during its construction, was the single largest cotton mill building in existence, at over one thousand feet long and five stories high.

Because Bailey refused to patent his invention for many years, rightly fearing that others around the country would copy his valuable machine, there were only a few power knitting mills in New York State as late as 1850.

Once Bailey patented his machines two years later, the knitting industry grew rapidly. In the years that followed, more than two dozen knitting mills were in operation at any given time in Cohoes, employing thousands of people. The Tivoli Mills on Mohawk Street alone employed five hundred operatives, while the Ranken Knitting Company on Erie Street employed four hundred and the Enterprise Mill on Courtland Street employed another two hundred.

In the year that Bailey and Egberts arrived to open their knitting mill, Cohoes was a tiny hamlet of only twenty houses. Thereafter, the population of Cohoes grew rapidly as a direct result of the new industry, so that the hamlet was quickly incorporated as a village in 1848 and as a city in 1869. The vast majority of the population derived its livelihood either directly or indirectly from the knitting mills.

The revolutionary invention of Timothy Bailey was only the first of many innovations made in and around Cohoes for improved knitting machinery. Luke Kavanaugh of nearby Waterford invented a rotary knitting burr that was quickly adopted by knitting machine manufacturers around the country. Business owners from the firms of Campbell and Clute and the Tompkins Brothers Machine Shop were also noted inventors, but they represent only a small portion of the total number in the Capital District who materially advanced the industry.

TIMOTHY BAILEY, ALBANY

Power Knitting Loom

The art of knitting is relatively new considering that humans have clothed themselves for many thousands of years. The first knit clothing made an appearance in Europe about 1560, possibly in the palace of England's Queen Elizabeth. This was a major breakthrough, as only knitted cloth has the elasticity that makes clothing as comfortable as it is today. For about thirty years, all knitting was done by hand until an Englishman named William Lee devised the first knitting machine. Although it was large, expensive and slow, there were very few improvements made upon it for over two hundred years, despite the efforts of dozens of inventors. Vast sums of money and great efforts were expended around Europe to improve upon the machine, which required a muscular man who had been thoroughly trained in its use to power it. It would ultimately take an American living in Albany to improve upon the machine and add the provision of water power.

Timothy Bailey's power knitting loom resulted in Cohoes becoming an important knitting and textile center. Pictured is the mammoth Harmony Mill. *Courtesy of the Library of Congress.*

A man with the unusual name of Egbert Egberts owned a store with his brother Cornelius in Albany under the firm name C. and E. Egberts. During a casual conversation with his doctor in 1831, he mentioned his idea for reconfiguring the complicated machine with a simpler design so that it could be powered by water. The only obstacle was a lack of mechanical ability to carry out such a project. The doctor recommended Timothy Bailey, who was employed by a cabinetmaker but had shown capabilities for building machinery.

Egberts later visited Bailey and described what he wanted. Bailey thought it could be done and agreed to give it a try if Egberts put up all of the capital. The two entered into a partnership and looked for a Lee machine on which to perform experiments. Since none could be found in Albany, Bailey traveled to Philadelphia and purchased an unused machine for fifty-five dollars. Within six days, he had found a way to operate it by a side crank, which was in itself a significant innovation. Egberts purchased a building at the foot of State Street for Bailey to continue his experiments. After many more months of effort, Bailey designed a machine that was able to make four shirt bodies and knit back and forth thirty times per minute.

The partners constructed more machines and set them up in a newly constructed cotton mill in Cohoes. Within a short time, the knitting mill had become the most successful in the country. The hand cranks on the machines were replaced with a means to power them by the water of Cohoes Falls. Where it previously took a person one day to knit two pairs of drawers with a hand loom, Bailey's power loom enabled a person to knit twenty pairs in the same time period. Since these were the first automated knitting machines in existence and had no patent protection, they were kept in a locked room with only a few trusted employees granted access. For about fifteen years, the knitting mill was the only one in the world where all shirt and drawer knitting was done by machinery.

Bailey's older brother, Joshua, and Egberts built a new knitting mill near Ontario and Remsen Streets in Cohoes, while Timothy Bailey continued to operate the original mill. Bailey suffered a setback in 1849 when the upper two floors of the mill were completely destroyed by fire. His losses totaled $5,000 in machinery, and two hundred employees were thrown out of work. Some of the machinery was salvaged, and Bailey decided to move his operations to Ballston Spa. It was there that he finally patented his knitting machine and, three years later, a powered rotary knitting machine.

The book *A History of American Manufacturers* states that of the 126 patents issued in the United States involving looms and knitting machinery, "the most valuable contribution to this class of textile machinery was that of Timothy Bailey, who was the first to give the world a Power Stocking Loom, having about the year 1852 succeeded in adapting the old improvements." The *Christian Advocate and Journal* even wrote an article about Bailey in 1856:

> *The world owes a debt of gratitude to God for the gifts he has bestowed upon those inventors who have by their genius contributed to the progress and elevation of humanity. There is a man now in America to whom the people are under inestimable obligation for his inventions and yet he has received but little pecuniary advantage, while others have been enriched by the products of his skill. The person to whom I refer is Mr. Timothy Bailey, now residing in Ballston Spa, the inventor of the first knitting machines in this country.*
>
> *His first machines were a wonderful advance upon former methods of knitting and are very extensively used. One of those machines will knit about 20,000 stitches per minute, 5,000 more than the one which excited the wonder of the writer of the Crystal Palace. This machine is straight and somewhat cumbersome and complicated. Mr. Bailey, some years after*

its invention, made considerable improvement upon it, simplifying and increasing its effectiveness. But in all probability the most wonderful thing in this line is his latest invention. He has recently constructed a rotary machine, quite simple in its movements, occupying about a third of the room of the old machine and requiring only about a third of the power to move it. It will knit a great variety of things, from a child's stocking up to a coat for a man. It will knit about 80,000 stitches per minute.

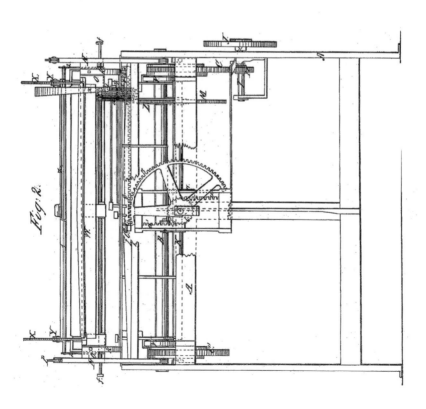

Timothy Bailey's "Knitting Machine."

Bailey's patent described the advantages of his machine over knitting by hand. Once the thread was stitched into the first row, no other attention was needed except to watch for breakages. As noted by the *Christian Advocate*, the greatly simplified machine increased the production per man-hour by up to 25 percent. He patented his rotary knitting machine three years later, which contained many of the same workings as the standard models but simplified the machinery for ease of use, repair and maintenance.

Joshua Bailey and Egbert Egberts amassed large fortunes as demand for their knit goods continued to increase. Timothy Bailey appears to have retired too early and was only left with $20,000. A few years after Joshua died in 1875, Timothy sued Joshua's adopted daughter for part of the inheritance and was awarded $775 per year from the estate. Despite succumbing to the fate of many famous inventors and living out the rest of his days in relative obscurity, his power knitting loom would later be remembered as one of the Capital District's most important inventions.

GEORGE CAMPBELL, COHOES

Winding Bobbin Machine

Soon after Timothy Bailey and Egbert Egberts decided to relocate from Albany to Cohoes with their new power knitting loom, Cohoes became known as the world's primary knitting center. For several years, the mill of Egberts and Bailey was the only knitting mill in the area, but in 1836, the Harmony Cotton Manufacturing Company was incorporated and went on to become the largest cotton mill ever built. By 1880, there were more than twenty-five knitting mills that employed more than four thousand operatives.

Dozens of innovations were developed in Cohoes to support the new industry. The firm of Campbell and Clute was one of several that manufactured improved machinery for the nearby mills. George Campbell was born in Montreal, Canada, on November 17, 1829, and educated in the district schools of nearby Cornwall. He came to Waterford in 1847 and apprenticed for three years as a machinist and eleven years as a journeyman. His first partnership was with noted foundry owner George Gage, which lasted for five years.

When his partnership with Gage came to an end, Campbell moved to Cohoes and formed a long-lasting partnership with businessman John Clute. Clute was born in Montgomery County on August 10, 1830. He

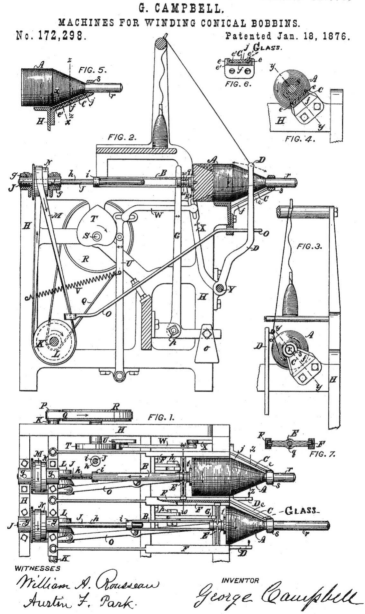

George Campbell's "Machine for Winding Conical Bobbins."

later came to Waterford and, like Campbell, worked in the machine shop of George Gage. He then moved on to the Cohoes Manufacturing Company for a few years before partnering with George Campbell. In 1863, the two men established a machine shop under the name Campbell and Clute on Mohawk Street in Cohoes. At first they made do with a two-story wooden building but later tore it down and built a four-story brick structure in its place. In the mid-1880s, the business employed fifty-five men and had an annual production of $100,000.

The firm prospered by manufacturing machinery for the burgeoning knitting industry in Cohoes and elsewhere around the country. Some of their products included double, flat rib and rotary knitting machines, seaming machines and knitting burrs. Most of their patent machinery was tested and used in the Massasoit Knitting Mills of the Munson Manufacturing Company, of which they were among the founders. The mills were located opposite the state dam in Cohoes and employed 125 people.

Campbell and Clute owned several patents that were filed separately by each partner or both together. One of their most successful products was the "Campbell Patent Winder," invented by Campbell in 1875. The machine consisted of a series of pulleys that powered a moveable conical bobbin for winding yarn. As the bobbin revolved, it was in constant contact with a sliding journal box that kept the yarn uniformly spaced and condensed for maximum efficiency. Clute alone patented a machine for uniting knit fabrics through the use of double-stitching. The partners together invented an upright rotary knitting machine that received an award at the 1876 International Exhibition for "an excellent attachment to prevent the work running off the needles when the thread breaks, and for good automatic self-regulating take-up."

Campbell was elected to the New York State Assembly in 1880 and was a delegate to the Chicago Convention four years later. The partnership of Campbell and Clute lasted twenty-five years and was only ended by Campbell's death in 1900. Clute continued on under the name Campbell and Clute Machine Company until his own death six years later.

LUKE KAVANAUGH, WATERFORD

Knitting Burr

Waterford's knitting and textile industry during the late 1800s and early 1900s was one of the most extensive in the history of Saratoga County, employing thousands of people. Among the largest were the Ford Manufacturing Company, the Eureka Knitting Mills, the Ormsby Textile Company, the Diamond Knitting Mills and the Himes Underwear Company, each of which gave employment to more than three hundred workers.

The largest and perhaps most successful of these textile companies was established and operated by Luke Kavanaugh and his sons. Kavanaugh was born in Ireland in 1830. He worked in several woolen mills around Leeds, England as a young boy, earning the equivalent of sixty-two cents per week. He and his young wife set sail for the United States soon after their son Charles was born in 1854. Arriving in New York City after six weeks at sea, the family made their way to Ottaway, Illinois, where four years later they would be on hand to witness the famous debate between Abraham Lincoln and Stephen Douglas. The family moved back east a few years later and settled in Waterford, where they remained for the rest of their lives. Luke found a job as a machinist with the firm Gage and Campbell.

While working in the Gage machine shop, Kavanaugh conceived the first of his several improvements in knitting burr blades. His 1862 patent letter described his rotary knitting burr with removable wings that were held stationary within "oblique radial slots in a hub by means of detachable wings, engaged with and clamped against the ends of the wings." This allowed an operator to easily change the wings for repair, replacement or to adapt the knitting machine for various types of material. His removable knitting burrs were a significant improvement over the fixed burrs used in other machines and were quickly adopted around the country.

Two more patents were submitted by Kavanaugh over the next two years, one for an improvement in blades for knitting machine sinkers and one for an improvement in knitting machinery. His next patent was filed in 1871, for an improvement in burrs for knitting machines consisting of a complete circular series of wings. This was an improvement on his first knitting burr, which employed separate detachable wings. His final knitting-related invention was easily his simplest, consisting of a knitting burr blade with a distinctive shape, although the patent letter did not specify the advantage of his blade over other blades used in knitting machines.

Finally deciding to make use of his inventions for his own profit, Kavanaugh and his son Charles established the Kavanaugh Knitting Company in 1886. It employed hundreds of people in Waterford and Cohoes and supplied all of the cotton undershirts used by the United States Army and Navy. A large, three-story brick building was constructed in 1891 to accommodate the growing business, and a year later the company was incorporated.

Another building was erected as a spinning plant to furnish the yarns that were used in the knitting factory. The additional building made it possible for the company to control all aspects of the clothing production cycle, from spinning the raw cotton into thread, to weaving the thread into cloth and finally to sewing the cloth into garments.

Kavanaugh's inventive mind conceived of ideas outside of the knitting industry as well. He patented a farming tractor to "devitalize or sterilize the germ and larval forms of animal life and the seeds of obnoxious plant life deposited on the surface of arable lands." His last patent was for an improved method of cooling castings to eliminate the "blow-holes, piping, and segregations" as the metal cooled. The curious contraption he devised for this purpose consisted of a series of pulleys, axles and piping that drew all of the gases out of the molten metal.

Kavanaugh passed away on January 24, 1909, only one year after his metal cooling patent was awarded, and left his wife with a substantial fortune from his successful knitting inventions. His two sons carried on the family business for another decade, but they decided to retire in 1920 and sell the business to the Goodyear Rubber Company.

CLARK TOMPKINS, COHOES

Upright Rotary Knitting Machine

Several entrepreneurs were able to operate long-lived and lucrative businesses by supporting the knitting mills of Cohoes and Troy, especially providing the machinery needed to produce the tons of clothing that were shipped daily. The Tompkins Brothers Machine Shop was perhaps the most successful of these. In 1906, the shop was described by the *Textile American* as "the oldest one of its kind in continuous existence on the American continent."

The company's founder was Clark Tompkins, born on July 10, 1808, in Little Compton, Rhode Island. In 1840, he moved his large family to Cohoes and began working as a machinist for the fledgling knitting industry. Four years later, he established a small shop on Congress Street in Troy, powered by a seventy-five-horsepower water wheel on the Poestenkill.

For the first few years, Tompkins manufactured looms for carpet and cotton mills, mill gearing and basic machinery. However, beginning in 1850, the output of the shop was expanded to include the many inventions that Tompkins began to design and patent. One of his earliest and most successful

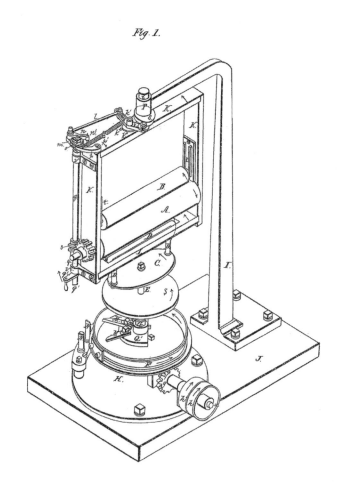

Clark Tompkins's "Knitting Machine."

inventions was the Upright Rotary Knitting Machine, patented with the help of gifted inventor John Johnson of Troy, with whom he collaborated on a number of knitting machine improvements. *The City of Troy and Its Vicinity* claims that the machine was "not surpassed by any other contrivance of its kind in its simplicity of construction and its adaptation to perfect the work for which it was so skillfully designed."

The superior design of the machine found a market not only in the many knitting mills of the Capital District but also throughout the United States, Canada and South America. The frame itself revolved in the same direction as the take-up mechanism and the needle cylinder to produce a more uniform and elastic knit cloth with very little human intervention and almost no noise. His winding bobbin machine automatically stopped when there was a break in the yarn, allowing an attendant to easily mend the yarn and resume its operation without having to adjust the bobbin.

The original wooden building was destroyed by fire in 1849, but Tompkins rebuilt the shop across the street with brick on a much larger scale, measuring 175 feet long by 45 feet wide. The business was incorporated under the name Empire Machine Company and operated as such until Clark Tompkins's death in 1877. His sons Albert and Ira assumed ownership of the business and thereafter operated under the name Tompkins Brothers.

The brothers continued the successful business for decades, as well as their father's tradition of patenting new machinery for production and sale. Ira began by patenting an improvement in machines for napping and brushing knitted fabrics in partnership with his father in 1873. Later, both of Clark's sons and a grandson named Ernest patented several dozen knitting machine improvements that were practical enough to produce and sell on the market. Advertisements in trade magazines boasted that the company was "a manufacturer and patentee of knitters, winders, washers, brushers, spoolers, stop motions, take-ups, and flock cutters." Ernest Tompkins became head of the Inventing Department, which contained a patent and technical library relating to all of the advances in the knitting industry. The business was later relocated to Syracuse and continues to manufacture knitting machinery to this day under the name Tompkins USA, Inc.

ARTS AND ENTERTAINMENT

The Capital District has historically been a center of popular cultural events and activities. Some of the most famous and long-lived venues of entertainment in the area include the Palace Theatre in Albany, Proctor's Theatre in Schenectady and the Cohoes Music Hall. They were built in the early 1900s and have hosted a variety of vaudeville, dance, orchestral and musical performances over the past century, but the area's cultural development dates back even further.

During the 1800s, Albany developed a sense of cultural achievement that went hand in hand with being the state's capital. Some of the city's most prominent industries bolstered that view, not least of which was the thriving and world-renowned piano industry. The Marshall and Wendell Piano-forte Manufacturing Company operated for decades on Broadway, employing seventy-five workmen and producing over six hundred pianos annually. Several other firms manufactured pianos, piano plates and piano hardware. However, the oldest and most successful firm was Boardman and Gray, which sold as many as 1,250 pianos per year. The business acumen of the partners certainly played a part in the success of the business, but the inventions of James Gray gave the firm an edge over other manufacturers, since the partners were able to offer improvements and features that no other firm could duplicate.

Albany's entertainment industry also achieved worldwide fame. In historical books of Albany, the manufacture of billiard balls is always highlighted. One might wonder just how such a unique industry would take root in the city and prosper for as long as it did. The answer is that

The Meneely foundry casting the Women's Liberty Bell for the suffragist movement in 1915. *Courtesy of the Library of Congress.*

the man who invented a new substance for coating billiard balls, John Hyatt, lived in Albany and organized a business to manufacture them. His company was incidentally considered to be the first successful plastics manufacturer in the world. Among Hyatt's other business enterprises was the Embossing Company, which produced patent dominoes, checkers and "Toys That Teach."

One of the region's greatest inventors, Henry Miller, was a music enthusiast who spent much of his time developing some of the early "talking machines" and "sound machines." Although his music inventions did not help establish or promote industry in the Capital District, since they were generally assigned to the Victor Talking Machine Company of New Jersey, many of his improvements were incorporated into phonographs that were sold around the world. However, the dozens of knitting machine inventions he patented were used by many of the area's textile mills.

Several other area inventors did their part in promoting the Capital District on a national stage. The bells of the Meneely family were produced by the thousands and shipped to churches and town governments around the world. When the famous Liberty Bell in Philadelphia was rendered unusable from a second crack, the Meneely family donated a Centennial

Bell to replace it so that it could be rung on the country's 100th birthday. The family owned two of the four bell foundries that operated in the Troy vicinity and patented many improvements for the manufacture of bells that helped them remain competitive.

The game of golf was turned on its head for a brief time after Arthur Knight of Schenectady introduced his improved putter in 1902. Few people with only one invention to their credit had one as famous as Knight did. The British were so upset about what they considered to be an unfair advantage given to its users that they banned the putter from professional play for fifty years.

JOHN HYATT, ALBANY

Celluloid for Billiard Balls

Rarely in American history did one inventor spawn more businesses on the strength of his inventions than John Wesley Hyatt. He not only established or was the inspiration for more than a half dozen successful manufacturing companies, but he also made one of the world's most important discoveries and, in the process, had a hand in saving an animal species from extinction.

The game of billiards has been popular for centuries, but by the mid-1800s, the problem of manufacturing enough billiard balls to keep up with demand had become increasingly difficult. The earliest balls were made of wood and later clay, but these were not ideal. Ivory began to be used as early as the sixteenth century and proved to be the most popular substance. However, elephants were in danger of becoming extinct as thousands were slaughtered for their tusks. Only about eight balls could be made from the tusks of one elephant.

Ivory became so expensive that a New York City manufacturing firm named Phelan and Collander offered a $10,000 prize to the person who could come up with the best alternative. This contest provided fresh incentive to inventor John Hyatt, who was at the time attempting to develop a better substance for making checkers and dominoes.

Hyatt was born on November 28, 1837, in Starky, New York, and received an education in the district schools of Yates County and the Eddytown Seminary. At the age of sixteen, he moved to Illinois with his older brother Isaiah and became a printer. There, he patented his first invention, a knife sharpener. After eleven years, he moved to Albany and

John Hyatt (1837–1920).
New York State Archives.

initially continued his career as a printer but soon turned his attention to manufacturing game pieces.

According to popular belief, one day Hyatt went to the cupboard in search of collodion (pyroxylin mixed with alcohol) for a cut on his hand. The bottle had tipped over, and the contents were spilled out and had become solidified. He noted that it was hard and elastic, which gave him new ideas for his experiments with making billiard balls. Later he heard that an Englishman had attempted to force camphor and collodion to unite and form a solid but was unsuccessful.

Hyatt set up a workshop behind his landlady's boardinghouse and built a machine that could apply heat and pressure to various substances. He began experimenting with camphor and collodion and found that if they were put into a strong press they would unite and form a new substance, which he called "celluloid." In his tests, he found it to be hard, lightweight and tough, and it could be dyed, heated, stamped or molded into a variety of forms. His 1869 patent described what is considered to be the first industrial man-made plastic and, therefore, is one of the country's most important patents of the nineteenth century. The patent did not mention the word "celluloid," but it has since become part of the English language. He obtained United States Trademark No. 1,102 on celluloid in 1873.

Because the mixture was flammable in its first iteration, it was not ideal for making billiard balls. One drawback was found when a lighted cigar was applied to a ball and it burst into flame. Another account contends that occasionally "the violent contact of the balls would produce a mild explosion like a percussion gun cap." One billiard saloon owner in Colorado wrote to Hyatt that he did not mind the volatility of the new balls but they could be dangerous at times, as the sound caused every patron in the room to draw their weapon.

The fate of Phelan and Collander's $10,000 prize remains a mystery (it is likely that the prize was never awarded). However, the new mixture was ideal for many other uses, such as card cases, buttons, eyeglass frames, hairpins, mirror backs, piano keys, toy dolls, dentures and drawer knobs. In the late 1880s, celluloid was applied to manufacturing photographic film, paving the way for film to replace photographic plate. In the first part of the twentieth century, it was adopted for use in making shirt cuffs, ballpoint pen bodies and knife handles.

Upon patenting his invention, Hyatt was quick to make use of it. Pure inventors are rarely good businessmen, but Hyatt proved to be equally talented in both fields. After refining the celluloid mixture to become less volatile, he started the Albany Billiard Ball Company on Delaware Avenue. This company is credited by most sources to be the first successful plastics manufacturing firm in history, since Hyatt was not only able to invent the substance itself but design the machinery to produce it as well. Two years later, he established the Albany Dental Plate Company to manufacture dentures from his new material. He created an improved dental plate using a pyroxyline mixture that he perfected and an apparatus for quickly molding the plates using a flask clamp and heating vessel. When the product line was expanded, the name of the company was changed to the Celluloid Manufacturing Company.

Continuing with his first love of producing game pieces, Hyatt patented an improved method for manufacturing dominoes that involved pressing a block of wood in a suitable mold. The mold created the cavities for the center

UNITED STATES PATENT OFFICE.

JOHN W. HYATT, JR., OF ALBANY, NEW YORK, AND ISAIAH S. HYATT, OF ROCKFORD, ILLINOIS.

IMPROVED METHOD OF MAKING SOLID COLLODION.

Specification forming part of Letters Patent No. 91,341, dated June 15, 1869.

To all whom it may concern:

Be it known that we, JOHN W. HYATT, Jr., of the city of Albany, in the State of New York, and ISAIAH S. HYATT, of the city of Rockford, in the State of Illinois, have invented a new and useful Method of Making Solid Collodion, or compounds of pyroxyline; and we do hereby declare the following specification to be a true and exact description of the nature of our invention.

Our convention consists of a new and improved method of manufacturing solid collodion and its compounds; its essential feature being the employment of a very small quantity of ether or other appropriate solvent, and dissolving pyroxyline therewith, under a heavy pressure, so that a comparatively hard and solid product is obtained, with great economy of solvents and saving of time.

The following description will enable others skilled in the art to use our process:

We place soluble cotton, pyroxyline, or prepared cellulose into a strong cylinder or suitably-shaped mold. With the pyroxyline may be mixed ivory-dust, bone-dust, asbestus, flake-white, or any other desirable substance, according to the nature of the product required.

This compound is then pressed into a tolerably compact mass by means of a plunger in the cylinder, or by a movable part of the mold. The plunger to said cylinder or part of the mold is then retracted to give room for the ether or other solvent. The proportion of solvent to the pyroxyline is as five to ten, seven to ten, or equal parts, by weight, according to the nature and proportions of the compound. When the pyroxyline is used alone, from one-half to three-fourths, by weight, of solvent will be sufficient; but when ivory-dust or other material is added, a somewhat greater proportion of solvent will be required, which can readily be determined by trial. After the plunger to the cylinder or part of the mold has been retracted, as aforesaid, the solvent is poured or forced in through a hole, which is then closed, and the plunger or movable part of the mold is immediately forced against the contents with great power—a pressure of from five to twenty tons per square inch being required to produce the best results. The pressure must be applied quickly, so that the solvent will be forced into contact with every particle of the pyroxyline before the dissolving process has time to commence. This, however, may be varied according to the degree of activity of the solvent employed. The cylinder or mold must be made or packed to work so closely that none of the solvent can escape the pressure. Other mechanical means may be employed equivalent to the foregoing, and we do not confine ourselves to the precise apparatus described.

The product is then taken out of the cylinder or mold, and will be found to be hard and solid, of uniform quality throughout, and liable to only a very slight degree of shrinkage, because of the very small proportion of volatile elements which it contains.

After the solid compound thus formed is taken out of the cylinder or mold, and before it thoroughly seasons, we subject it, in the manufacture of many articles, to additional pressure in molds, whereby it is caused to conform perfectly with all the configurations of the mold.

Having thus described our invention, what we claim, and desire to secure by Letters Patent, is—

1. Dissolving pyroxyline under pressure, substantially as described.

2. Dissolving pyroxyline under pressure, when combined with ivory-dust or other material, substantially as described.

JOHN W. HYATT, Jr.
ISAIAH S. HYATT.

Witnesses:
HENRY DEITZ,
C. M. HYATT.

John Hyatt's "Improved Method of Making Solid Collodion."

line and spots for the domino. The Embossing Company was established on the strength of this patent alone but over time expanded to manufacture a variety of toys and games. Using the slogan "Toys That Teach," the company's catalogue featured building kits containing levers, beams, axles, pulleys and bolts. Another patent filed by Hyatt and his brothers Isaiah and Charles was for an apparatus that could quickly enamel racks of checkers using a revolving wheel.

Not content to discover one substance, in 1878 Hyatt discovered bonsilate, which he made from bones and silica. The new substance was hard, elastic and capable of being dyed any color. In that year, he organized the Bonsilate Company on the corner of Church and Pruyn Streets, where he employed twenty men. Hyatt was listed as "Expert" among the other officers of the company. Bulk quantities of bonsilate were shipped all over the country to firms that previously used ivory, amber or coral in their manufacturing process.

Unable to find sufficient capital in Albany to adequately fund the growth of his plastics venture, Hyatt moved the Celluloid Manufacturing Company to Newark, New Jersey, in 1873. The Albany Billiard Ball Company and Embossing Company remained in Albany and continued operating for many years. Businessman Peter Kinnear assumed control of the Albany Billiard Ball Company in 1875, although Hyatt remained as vice-president. The Embossing Company employed about one hundred workers until it was sold to Halsam Products of Chicago in 1955. In New Jersey, Hyatt continued to issue new inventions, such as an anti-friction roller bearing, a multi-stitch sewing machine, a machine for making school blackboards and a water purifier. Based on these and other inventions, he started the Hyatt Pure Water Company, the Hyatt Roller Bearing Company, the Newark Filtering Company and the New Jersey Wick Company.

Although Hyatt moved to New Jersey in 1873 and spent the rest of his life there, his earliest and most important inventions were developed in Albany, and several of the businesses he founded and supported with his patents operated in that city until the late 1900s. He was one of the area's most prolific inventors—various sources credit him with at least two hundred patents. He received the Perkin Medal of Honor from the Society of Chemical Industry for his work in developing celluloid and was inducted into the National Inventors Hall of Fame. He passed away on May 10, 1920, at the age of eighty-four.

James Gray, Albany

Piano Attachment

William Boardman was a wholesale grocer in Albany and had no desire to conduct any other type of business. However, he agreed to endorse the piano factory of a friend in 1836, and when that friend defaulted on his loans, Boardman discovered that he was the new owner. Luckily, a local man named James Gray was manufacturing pianos on a small scale and agreed to come work for him. Two years later, Gray became a partner and helped make the business highly successful.

Gray was born in New York City in 1815. After receiving a good education in the public schools, he went to work for piano makers Firth and Hall, where he learned to tune pianos. After moving to Albany in 1825, he established the city's first piano manufacturing shop. Upon joining Boardman's firm, he concentrated on the manufacturing side of the business, which was crucial in developing a reputation for quality instruments.

Over the years, the small company was built up into a world-class piano factory. The complexity of constructing these instruments is illustrated by the fact that twenty-three different departments were required to produce each piano. By 1860, about twenty-five pianos were shipped each week to all parts of the United States and Canada. Nearly two hundred pianos were in the process of being built on any given day.

After joining with Boardman, Gray began experimenting with different manufacturing techniques and sounds that led to his invention of the Dolce Campana in 1848. A rack containing heavy weights was held in a frame over the bridge. Pushing a pedal would allow the weights to drop against screws inserted in the bridge, producing a vibrato effect. A variety of sounds could be made by striking chords and adjusting the pedal slightly so the weights were either lightly resting on the bridge or applying their full weight. Although it would seem that a piano would not be able to take this punishment very well, several independent reviews testified that no damage was caused after years of use. Over one thousand of these thirty-dollar devices were attached to pianos at the request of customers.

A patent for Gray's Dolce Campana was awarded in Great Britain and apparently caused considerable excitement in the industry. In one review, *Music World* stated that "it has been his peculiar fortune to attain a European as well as an American reputation, and to win concurrent testimony favorable to his manufactures from musical critics, who generally are not remarkable for their unanimity of sentiment."

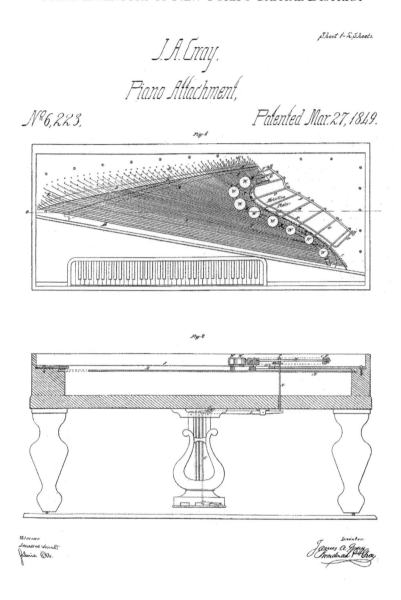

James Gray's "Pianoforte."

Gray was a prolific inventor with a variety of patented and unpatented improvements to pianos. An 1851 patent was filed for an "independent oscillating shoulder" to act upon in throwing the hammer against the strings to create new sounds. He patented a "Corrugated Sounding Board" in

1855, claiming that the new board provided more sounding surface and additional stiffness without the need to glue bars on either side. It was said that the board made the pianoforte sound more like a grand piano. Another patent utilized a single casting of iron for the upper sides, front and back of the piano case in order to simplify production. In addition to his "formal improvements," Gray made many other unpatented improvements to his pianos. For example, certain parts of the instrument were made of iron rather than traditional wood material to prevent warping.

In 1866, Gray purchased Boardman's share of the business but retained the old name in deference to his longtime partner. A few years later, Gray took his sons William and James Jr. into the business, who inherited it upon Gray's death in 1889. By that time, the firm was well known as one of the oldest piano manufacturing firms in the country. The long-lived business shut down in 1926 after almost a century of operation.

HENRY MILLER, WATERFORD

Sound Machines

As Saratoga County's greatest inventor, Henry Miller was one of the few men in the Capital District to make a living in that occupation alone, selling dozens of patents to various businesses around Troy and the Victor Talking Machine Company of New Jersey. The scope of his inventing career is staggering—a collection of his varied and often complex patents fills a thick book at the Waterford Museum and Cultural Center in Waterford.

Miller was born on April 10, 1869, in Fort Wayne, Indiana. Deprived of a formal education as a child, he acquired all of his mechanical knowledge while working with his father, who was a contractor and bridge builder for the Wabash Railroad. When still in his teens, Miller decided to travel the country doing odd jobs before boarding a ship bound for Europe and Africa. Upon returning home, he went to work with his brother at the Fort Wayne Pneumatic Novelty and Model Works. It was there that he began his career as an inventor.

In 1900, he decided to settle in Upstate New York and outfit a modern, well-equipped machine shop in which he created his many inventions. When he had an idea or encountered a mechanical puzzle, he would sit quietly for an hour or two and work it out in his head. Then he would begin to make rough sketches of his idea on paper laid out on the floor. From these he would create patterns and models, and the quest for the ideal solution would begin.

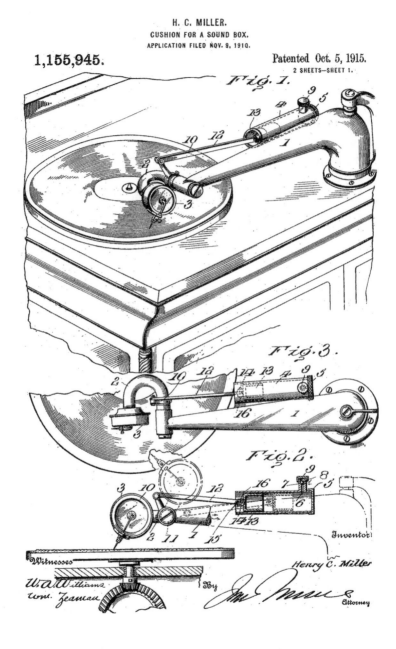

H. C. MILLER.
CUSHION FOR A SOUND BOX.
APPLICATION FILED NOV. 9, 1910.

1,155,945.

Patented Oct. 5, 1915.
2 SHEETS—SHEET 1.

Fig. 1.

Fig. 3.

Fig. 2.

Inventor
Henry C. Miller
By
Attorney

Witnesses
W. A. Williams
Wm. Zeaman

Henry Miller's "Cushion for a Sound Box."

His first patent was a collar-trimming machine, filed on July 9, 1901. This was clearly inspired by the success of the collar and cuff industry of nearby Troy, which even at the turn of the century maintained the lead in the manufacture of those articles. Miller filed dozens of patents in this field and sold the rights to various textile manufacturers in the area, such as his button-hole machines, thread-cutting devices, collar dies, fabric starching methods and dampening machines.

Over the course of his inventing career, Miller patented a wide variety of sound-boxes and sound-box improvements, many of which were sold to the Victor Talking Machine Company of Camden, New Jersey. Some of the patent titles were: "Combined Stand and Horn for Talking Machines," "Motor For Talking Machines," "Tone Arm Mounting For Sound Reproducing Machines," "Cushion For Sound-Box" and "Cabinet Sound Reproducing Machine." He experimented extensively with pneumatic principles and how they could be applied to phonographs. One such experiment involved two tin bath tubs clamped together, which led to the development of a curved horn of galvanized iron that could catch and amplify sounds without distortion. The compression of the airwaves in the horn took the place of the vibrating diaphragm used in other machines.

One phonograph manufacturer named the Cletor Company was so impressed by Miller's innovations that it used them in its production line. Miller soon found out about this patent violation and sued for damages. After several years of litigation, he forced Cletor to pay him thousands of dollars for the rights to his patents. The Victor Talking Machine Company took the legal route from the onset and purchased many of Miller's patents.

Such was his interest in music that Miller created what he called a "grandphonium" for his home, said to reproduce ordinary musical records better than any other sound machine in existence. It was powered by compressed air and contained attachments that had never been used before. *New York Times* publisher Adolph Ochs marveled at the machine and suggested that Miller display it for the public, but it was considered to be Miller's greatest treasure and he was reluctant to give it up.

Miller was blessed throughout much of his life with good health and a strong constitution. However, in his late fifties he developed a heart condition that plagued him for the remainder of his years and would lead to a fatal heart attack on August 28, 1930. His shop was converted to the Miller Apartments, where his son Chester worked as custodian. The fact that Henry Miller patented more inventions than the next top five Saratoga County inventors combined is testament to his unique talent and imagination.

THE MENEELY FAMILY, TROY AND WATERVLIET

Bells and Bell Fixtures

During the late 1800s, the Troy-Watervliet area was considered the bell capital of the world. Its four bell manufacturers sold a combined total of more than 100,000 bells to every continent except Antarctica. Dozens of medals, premiums and honors were awarded to the Meneely family for their bells, including the Gold Medal of the American Institute of New York for the first complete chime of bells produced in America.

The foundry operated by Andrew Meneely was both the most successful and the longest-running bell foundry in the Capital District. The Meneely family emigrated from Ireland in the late 1700s and settled in Gibbonsville (the hamlet of Gibbonsville was renamed West Troy in 1836 and Watervliet in 1896). A son named Andrew was born on May 19, 1802. At the age of sixteen, he became apprenticed at the factory of Julius Hanks, who operated the first foundry in the Capital District for manufacturing bells and mathematical instruments. This experience laid the groundwork for the long-lived and successful business that followed.

After a brief time working for Horatio Hanks at Auburn, New York, Andrew returned to West Troy and took over the Julius Hanks foundry when the latter moved to Troy. With a small amount of capital, Meneely worked hard and built up the business so that within ten years it was the largest bell foundry in the country. His eldest son, Edwin, joined the firm in 1849, taking full charge of the finances and administration. His second son, George, was admitted when he came of age and took charge of the foundry.

George Rodney Meneely was born on March 15, 1831, in West Troy and was educated at the Jonesville Academy, Saratoga County. When his father Andrew died, George and his brother Edwin assumed ownership of the business, which became known as Andrew Meneely's Sons. By that time, the manufacture of surveying instruments had been discontinued due to competition from W. and L.E. Gurley of Troy. However, the brothers expanded the bell-making side of the business by adding a large melting furnace and rebuilding the foundry.

Beginning in the 1860s, George began inventing and patenting a variety of bell-related improvements. These included "Improvements for Attaching Bells to Their Yokes," "Hanging Bells" and "Improvements in Chimes and Alarms." The company claimed that its "Conical Rotary Yoke, patented in 1860 and 1868, is in all respects the most desirable church bell hanger

Clinton Hanks Meneely (1839–1923), *far right*, with his son Chester and grandson Clinton. *Courtesy of the Meneely family.*

in use." Various church bell fixtures were protected under four patents. Since George had charge of the manufacturing arm of the foundry, he not only was able to recognize improvements needed for hanging, ringing or manufacturing bells, but he could then implement his improvements into the assembly line as well.

George left the bell foundry in 1874 and established the George R. Meneely and Company foundry on South Albany Street near the Watervliet Arsenal. The sole purpose of the company was to manufacture his patented journal bearings for railroad cars and locomotives. The demand for this invention was so great that he established a second foundry in Atlanta, Georgia, to serve southern markets. He then established the Meneely Hardware Company with John Gibbons in 1883. Gibbons was also an inventor who had dozens of patents for such diverse items as tools, bicycles, axles, snap-hooks and roller bearings.

A third brother named Clinton spent a few years working in the family bell foundry but chose to enlist in the army at the outbreak of the Civil War. The rest of the family was opposed to this, which created a rift when he returned home. The two older brothers refused to let him back into the family business, so he crossed the Hudson River into Troy and started the Clinton H. Meneely Foundry with his brother-in-law George Kimberly. This also proved to be a highly successful enterprise, which alone manufactured twenty-five thousand bells, including the replacement Liberty Bell in Philadelphia and the Women's Liberty Bell on behalf of the suffragist movement. Customers were located throughout North America, South America, Asia, Africa, Europe and Australia.

Clinton Meneely's firm made a specialty of proper bell mountings, claiming that its rotary bell mountings were the most efficient in the world. He was awarded a patent for a bell-yoke attachment in 1871, the object of which was to "secure the clapper in its proper position with reference to the swinging of the bell under all circumstances," as well as providing a means to easily change the position of the bell and clapper to spread the wear to other parts of the mechanism, prolonging its life.

GEORGE R. MENEELY.

Improvement in Chime Alarm and other Bells.

No. 122,397.   Patented Jan. 2, 1872.

George Meneely's "Improvement in Chime, Alarm and Other Bells."

Meanwhile the original bell foundry in Watervliet manufactured over forty thousand bells that were shipped around the United States, Mexico, the West Indies and South America. In the 1870s, more than ninety different types of church, academy, factory, plantation and depot bells were offered for sale in weights ranging from one hundred pounds to three tons. Smaller bells were designed for ships, steamboats and locomotives. About 350 chimes (consisting of eight or more bells) and several carillons (consisting of twenty-three or more bells) were also sold. The two Meneely foundries manufactured 65 percent of all chimes and were the only American companies to manufacture carillons, considered to be the apex of achievement in bell making.

The family rift between Clinton and his brothers was reportedly mended in the 1940s, but not before the three brothers had died. Edwin was the first to pass away in 1887. George Meneely followed on October 23, 1915, at the age of eighty-four. Clinton Meneely, the youngest brother, passed away on July 1, 1923, also at the age of eighty-four. Both the Clinton Meneely Bell Company and the Meneely Bell Company lasted well into the 1900s. During and after World War II, a combination of metal shortages and the increasing popularity of electronic chimes finally led to the closure of both factories in 1952. Although the bell foundries of the Meneely family were shut down over a half century ago, thousands of their bells still ring in the Capital District and around the world.

ARTHUR KNIGHT, SCHENECTADY

The Schenectady Putter

Chances are, if you or someone you know has a golf memorabilia collection, among the clubs will be found a Schenectady Putter. The famous golf club was used by Walter Travis to secure the first American win in the British Amateur Championship in 1904, upsetting the British so much that they banned it from play for fifty years.

Its inventor, Arthur F. Knight, worked as an engineer at the General Electric plant in Schenectady. Although only an occasional golfer at first, by the time the Mohawk Golf Club was formed in 1898 he had become an enthusiast. Others were content just to "make the team," but after much practice, Knight became the best golfer in the club. He was so competitive that the prospect of losing his number one position caused Knight much anxiety. Believing that his game suffered several weaknesses, he set his mind to creating a putter that would help him maintain his ranking.

After some experimentation, he created a putter in 1902 that featured the shaft inserted into the center of a flat-sided head. He first made a wooden model and brought it to the club with him, planning to practice with it in anticipation of a tournament in Syracuse. After watching Knight practice for a while, club president S.M. Hamill remarked, "If you can't play golf without using such a thing as that, we don't need you tomorrow." Knight was forced to leave the club behind and ended up losing the match.

Upon returning home, he began designing one of his putters out of aluminum. His first attempt failed, but on the second attempt he created a club that became the final design. It had a shaft inclination of twenty-five degrees, a long striking face and a centered design for greater overall balance. While confident of the club's merits, he hoped to get an expert opinion. Coincidently, golfer Devereux Emmet of Garden City was visiting the Mohawk Gold Club a short time after Knight constructed his putter and agreed to give it a try. Returning to the clubhouse later in the day, Knight found a note from Emmet saying that he had to leave but had taken the putter with him for further study.

A few days later, Knight received a surprise telegram from the most successful amateur golfer in the country, Walter Travis. Emmet had played a few rounds with Travis and showed him Knight's putter. Travis was so impressed that he asked Knight to make one for him. Knight sent a putter that had a bit more loft, and after using it, Travis responded that it was "the best putter I have ever used." The icing on the cake came when Travis used the putter during the U.S. Open Championship and came in second. Within a week, Knight had received letters from over one hundred prominent golfers who requested "a putter like Mr. Travis'."

Knight was unprepared for such a response and did not even have a name for the new putter. At first he proposed calling it the "Travis Putter," but Travis suggested calling it the "Schenectady Putter." Travis went on to use the putter to win the U.S. Amateur tournament in 1903 and, in a stunning upset, was the first American to win the British Amateur the following year. Perhaps in response to this "humiliating" loss, the Royal and Ancient Golf Club Committee banned all "center-shafted, mallet-headed implements" in 1910, and although the United States Golf Association did not follow suit, the ruling limited its use in professional play. Still, it was widely used in the United States and was even endorsed by President William Taft.

Despite patenting his putter, manufacturers around the country almost immediately began selling similar, if not identical, golf clubs. Knight created the Schenectady Putter Company and had some success, but marketing

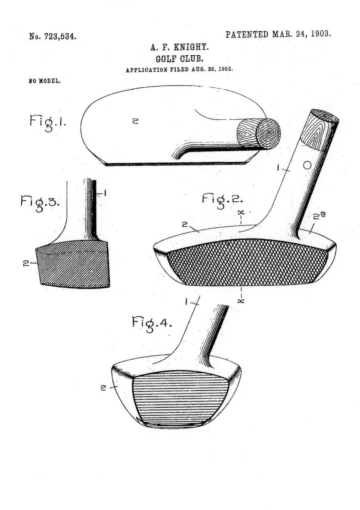

No. 723,534.

PATENTED MAR. 24, 1903.

A. F. KNIGHT.
GOLF CLUB.
APPLICATION FILED AUG. 26, 1902.

NO MODEL.

Fig.1.

Fig.3.

Fig.2.

Fig.4.

Witnesses:

by

Inventor:
Arthur F. Knight,

Att'y.

Arthur Knight's "Golf Club."

giants such as Spalding and the Standard Golf Company had advantages that were difficult to overcome. Today, the Schenectady Putter is a collector's item. The original putter used by Travis was purchased by the Garden City Golf Club in 1918 and reverently displayed for over thirty years, but it was stolen in 1951 and never returned.

CONTENTS BY TOWN

ALBANY

COHOES

LANSINGBURGH

SCHENECTADY

TROY

WATERFORD

Contents by Town

WATERVLIET

BIBLIOGRAPHY

Backus, Rev. J. Trumbull. *Address at the Funeral of the Rev. Dr. Nott*. New York: Press of Wynkoop and Hallenbeck, 1866.

Bennett, John. *Union University Quarterly* 3, no. 1. Schenectady: Union College, 1906.

Bergh, Albert. *The Writings of Thomas Jefferson, Volume XVII*. Washington, D.C.: Thomas Jefferson Memorial Association, 1907.

Bolles, Albert. *Industrial History of the United States*. Norwich, CT: Henry Hill Publishing Company, 1878.

The Brass World and Platers' Guide. Bridgeport, CT: December 1914.

Brown, Simon. *The New England Farmer, Volume VIII*. Boston: Joel Nourse, 1856.

Brown, Travis. *Historical First Patents: The First United States Patent for Many Everyday Things*. Metuchen, NJ: Scarecrow Press, 1994.

Butler, Joseph. *Fifty Years of Iron and Steel*. Cleveland, OH: Penton Press, 1922.

Byrn, Edward. *The Progress of Invention in the Nineteenth Century*. New York: Munn and Company, 1900.

Challoner, Jack. *1001 Inventions That Changed the World*. N.p.: Barron's Educational Series, 2009.

Cochrane, Robert. *The Romance of Industry and Invention*. London: W&R Chambers, Ltd., 1896.

Crisman, Kevin, and Arthur Cohn. *When Horses Walked on Water: Horse-powered Ferries in Nineteenth Century America*. Washington, D.C.: Smithsonian Institution Press, 1998.

Darrow, Floyd. *Masters of Science and Invention.* New York: Harcourt, Brace & Company, 1923.

Eberle, Irmengarde. *Famous Inventors.* New York: Dodd, Mead & Company, 1941.

The Empire State: Its Industries and Wealth. New York: American Publishing and Engraving Company, 1888.

Forster, John. *Collections and Researches Made by the Michigan Pioneer and Historical Society.* Lansing, MI: Robert Smith and Company, 1894.

Freedley, Edwin. *Leading Pursuits and Leading Men: A Treatise of the Principal Trades and Manufactures of the United States.* Philadelphia: Edward Young, 1856.

Gorowitz, Bernard. *The General Electric Story (Volumes 1-4).* Schenectady, NY: Schenectady Elfun Society, 1976.

Greenburg, Brian. *Worker and Community: Response to Industrialization in a Nineteenth-Century City, Albany, New York.* Albany: State University of New York Press, 1971.

Iles, George. *Leading Inventors.* New York: Henry Holt & Company, 1912.

Industrial Albany: Manufacturing and Distributing Advantages. Albany, NY: Industrial Bureau, Chamber of Commerce, 1930.

Jones, Thomas. *Journal of the Franklin Institute of the State of Pennsylvania, Volume III.* Philadelphia: Franklin Institute, 1831.

Keiper, Frank. *Pioneer Inventions and Pioneer Patents.* Rochester, NY: Pioneer Publishing Company, 1948.

Kirkman, Marshall. *The Compound Locomotive: Supplement to the Science of Railways.* New York: World Railway Publishing Company, 1899.

Lawler, James. *Modern Plumbing, Steam and Hot Water Heating.* New York: Popular Publishing Company, 1904.

McElroy, John. *Scotch-Irish McElroys in America.* Albany, NY: Brandow Printing Company, 1901.

Meneely and Company, Bell-Founders, West Troy, NY. Troy, NY: Weed, Parson and Company, 1876.

Monroe, Joel Henry. *Schenectady Ancient and Modern: A Complete and Connected History of Schenectady from the Granting of the First Patent in 1661 to 1914.* Albany, NY: Joel Henry, 1914.

Munsell, Howell. *History of the County of Schenectady, N.Y. from 1662 to 1886.* New York: W.W. Munsell and Company, 1886.

Nelson, James. *Reign of Iron: The Story of the First Battling Ironclads.* New York: HarperCollins Publishers, Inc., 2004.

Parker, Amasa. *Landmarks of Albany County, New York.* Syracuse, NY: D. Mason and Company, 1897.

Peterson, Julie. *Fiber Optics Illustrated Dictionary.* Boca Raton, FL: CRC Press LLC, 2003.

Portrait and Biographical Album of St. Joseph County, Michigan. Chicago: Chapman Brothers, 1889.

Prescott, George. *History, Theory, and Practice of the Electric Telegraph.* Boston: Ticknor and Fields, 1860.

Prout, Henry. *A Life of George Westinghouse.* New York: American Society of Mechanical Engineers, 1921.

Reynolds, Cuyler. *Albany Chronicles: A History of the City Arranged Chronologically.* Albany, NY: J.B. Lyon Company, 1906.

——. *Hudson-Mohawk Genealogical and Family Memoirs Volumes I–III.* New York: Lewis Historical Publishing Company, 1911.

The Schenectady Electrical Handbook. Schenectady, NY: American Institute of Electrical Engineers, 1904.

Silliman, Benjamin. *Electro-Magnetism: History of Davenport's Invention.* New York: C. & G. Carvill & Company, 1837.

Solomon, Brian. *American Steam Locomotive.* Osceola, WI: MBI Publishing, 1998.

Spafford, Horatio Gates. *A Gazetteer of the State of New York.* Albany, NY: H.C. Southwick, 1813.

Stone, William. *Manufacturers and Inventions of the United States.* New York: 1876.

Thompson, Silvanus. *Lectures on the Electromagnet.* New York: W.J. Johnston Company, 1891.

Transactions of the American Society of Heating and Ventilating Engineers, Volume XIII. New York: Society at the Office of the Secretary, 1907.

Usher, Abbott. *A History of Mechanical Inventions.* Boston: Beacon Press, 1929.

Van Santvoord, C. *Memoirs of Eliphalet Nott, D.D. L.L.D., for Sixty-Two Years President of Union College.* New York: Sheldon and Company, 1876.

Walton, Perry. *The Story of Textiles.* Boston: Walton Advertising & Printing Company, 1925.

Weise, Arthur James. *Troy's One Hundred Years 1789–1889.* New York: William H. Young, 1891.

Wendel, Charles. *Encyclopedia of American Farm Implements and Antiques.* Iola, WI: KP Krause Publications, 2004.

Westbrook, Jack. *Material Memories of the Mohawk-Hudson Region.* Fleischmanns, NY: Purple Mountain Press, 2007.

Williams, Archibald. *The Romance of Modern Invention.* London: C. Arthur Pearson, Ltd., 1903.

Winslow, John. *John Flack Winslow and the USS Monitor.* Poughkeepsie, NY: 1893.

Woods, Clinton. *Ideas That Became Big Business.* Baltimore, MD: Founders, Inc., 1959.

ABOUT THE AUTHOR

The author was born in Danbury, Connecticut, and moved with his family to Hebron, New York, in 1977. During his senior year in high school, he wrote his first book, a novel called *The Meatloaf Incident and Other Adventures* that is based on his experiences growing up in a rural community. He received a bachelor of science degree in accounting and a bachelor of arts degree in history from Castleton State College. He also received a master's degree in business administration from Chadwick University.

Soon after graduating college, he moved to the historic county of Saratoga. After noticing many ruins around the town of Milton, he began researching its history, particularly during the mid- to late 1800s. After stumbling upon the old trolley railroad bed behind his house, he was motivated to write a book about it, called *The Ballston Terminal Railroad and Its Successors*. That project naturally led to another one that detailed the industries served by the railroad, called *Lost Industries of the Kaydeross Valley*. When he discovered that several important inventions were developed to support these industries, yet another project unfolded that resulted in a Ballston Spa book of inventions and a Saratoga County book of inventions. His two biographies cover the lives of local industrialists George West and Isaiah Blood.

He is a featured writer in Ann Hauprich's book *Legacies Unlimited* in a chapter titled "Timothy Starr: He (Literally) Wrote the Book on Village Inventors." In 2009, he contributed an essay about Saratoga County inventors for the Brookside Museum's book *In Our Own Words: The Story of Saratoga County*. He has also been published in *Saratoga Living, Our Towne*

Ballston Spa, Spotlight Milton, the *Saratogian*, *Schenectady Gazette* and the *Ballston Journal* and is a frequent contributor to the *Ballston Spa Life* History Lesson series. He is currently the treasurer of the Saratoga County Historical Society (Brookside) Board of Trustees, and he lives in Rock City Falls with his wife, Alison, and daughter, Morgan.